10.60

G4

THROUGH A
DARKENING GLASS

By the Same Author

The Concept of Prayer
Faith and Philosophical Enquiry
Death and Immortality
Moral Practices (with H. O. Mounce)
Sense and Delusion (with Ilham Dilman)
Athronyddu Am Grefydd
Religion Without Explanation
Dramau Gwenlyn Parry
Belief, Change and Forms of Life

THROUGH A DARKENING GLASS

Philosophy, Literature, and Cultural Change

D. Z. Phillips

BASIL BLACKWELL
OXFORD

© 1982 by University of Notre Dame Press

First published in the United Kingdom in 1982.
Basil Blackwell Publisher
108 Cowley Road
Oxford OX4 1JF
England

British Library Cataloguing in Publication Data
Phillips, D.Z.
    Through a darkening glass.
    1. Literature—Philosophy—Addresses, essays, lectures
    I. Title
    808'.001   PN45
    ISBN 0-631-12995-2

Manufactured in the United States of America

To
David Sims

Philosophy, religion, science, they are all of them busy nailing things down, to get a stable equilibrium . . . But the novel, no . . . If you try to nail anything down, in the novel, either it kills the novel, or the novel gets up and walks away with the nail.

D. H. LAWRENCE

CONTENTS

ACKNOWLEDGMENTS   ix

1 / INTRODUCTION:
THROUGH A DARKENING GLASS   1

2 / ALLEGIANCE AND CHANGE IN MORALITY
—*A Study in Contrasts*   9

3 / SOME LIMITS TO MORAL ENDEAVOR   30

4 / MORAL PRESUPPOSITIONS
AND LITERARY CRITICISM   51

5 / PHILOSOPHIZING AND READING A STORY   64

6 / WHAT THE COMPLEX DID TO OEDIPUS   82

7 / KNOWLEDGE, PATIENCE, AND FAUST   89

8 / MEANING, MEMORY, AND LONGING   113

9 / INGMAR BERGMAN'S REDUCTIONISM
—*"A Modern Cosmology of the Spirit"*   133

10 / SEEKING THE POEM IN THE PAIN
—*Order and Contingency
in the Poetry of R. S. Thomas*   165

PHILOSOPHICAL BIBLIOGRAPHY   191

LITERARY BIBLIOGRAPHY   193

INDEX   195

ACKNOWLEDGMENTS

FOUR OF THE NINE ESSAYS in this collection are published here for the first time and a fifth is not readily accessible.

"Meaning, Memory, and Longing" was written during a visit to the Perkins School of Theology at the Southern Methodist University, Dallas, at Easter, 1979. "The Reductionism of Ingmar Bergman" was delivered as two lectures in a Bergman Film Week-End at the University College of Swansea in the Easter Term of 1980. "What the Complex Did to Oedipus" was given as a talk for the B.B.C. on Radio 3 on February 20th, 1979. "Seeking the Poem in the Pain" was given as a lecture in the Dylan Thomas Summer School at the University College of Swansea in 1977. "Some Limits to Moral Endeavor" was my inaugural lecture, published by the University College of Swansea in November, 1971.

The remaining essays were published as follows: "Philosophizing and Reading a Story" in *Sense and Delusion* by Ilham Dilman and D. Z. Phillips, Routledge and Kegan Paul, 1971; "Allegiance and Change in Morality; A Study in Contrasts" in *Philosophy and the Arts*, Royal Institute Lectures Vol. 6, 1971/72, edited by G. Vesey, Macmillan & Co., 1973; "Knowledge, Patience and Faust" in *The Yale Review*, Spring 1980. The last was written for a University of Wales Extra-Mural Conference on the Faust legend in June, 1978.

I am grateful to all concerned for permission to use the previously published material here. I am also grateful for the care with which the secretary of the Department of Philosophy, Mrs. Valerie Gabe, has typed the unpublished material. My thanks are also due to Mr. D. M. Evans who kindly helped me with the proofreading. Finally may I thank the anonymous reader for the University of Notre Dame Press from whose criticisms and suggestions I benefited a great deal.

Swansea,   D. Z. Phillips
January 1981.

1 /INTRODUCTION
THROUGH A DARKENING GLASS

THE CHOICE OF TITLE for this collection of essays, *Through A Darkening Glass*, is meant to reflect two themes which run through the essays. First, the main concern in many of the essays is to try to understand how moral and other perspectives on life may change, be eroded, be found wanting, or become impossible for people. The glass which was once clear darkens for them. How is this phenomenon or, rather, cluster of phenomena to be understood? A conviction running through these essays is that philosophy has a central role to play in answering this question. On the other hand, attempts at philosophical analysis can go either way: they can obscure as well as clarify. Here is the second reference to the darkening glass. Philosophy itself may be such a mirror, and what it obscures, in that event, is the ways in which modes of thought may become obscure for people. This can be brought out powerfully, it seems to me, by using literature as a source of reminders (not examples) from which philosophy can benefit in wrestling with issues concerning the firm or slackening hold of various perspectives in human life.

The second essay in the collection is described as "a study in contrasts." The contrasts referred to are those between philosophical theories about morality on the one hand and, on the other hand, what literature can show about the phenomena which those philosophical theories claim to clarify and explain. As we have said, the phenomena in question are the ways in which certain perspectives become darkening mirrors for people. Certain theories which have dominated moral philosophy make such perspectival changes, not only obscure, but impossible. According to these theories, the distinction between the rational and the irrational is unproblematic. Reason constitutes a unity. With this unquestioned assumption in the background, it is claimed that we have reasons for our values, reasons for changing our values. It seems to follow that, apart from slips, miscalculations, or inexperience, when our values change we are becoming more reasonable. On a social level, the picture is one of society becoming more and more rational as it sheds its inhibitions and taboos. On a strict interpretation of these views, there can be no darkening glass, no loss or erosion of what is worthwhile. We are simply shedding what is irrational as we make our slow but inevitable progress.

When we turn from these philosophical theories to look at what striking literary works portray so powerfully, a very different picture awaits us. To study the novels of Edith Wharton in this context is particularly appropriate, since she is concerned with the decline of traditional perspectives and values in the New York of the late nineteenth century. By studying her writings we can see that we do not have reasons for our values, but that our values are our reasons. When these values are changed or eroded, it is not because they have been shown to be mistaken according to a common conception of rationality, but because they have been affected by the coming of, and contact with, values of another kind.

In the third essay an attempt is made to show how the rationalism and optimism of these theories which characterize moral change as progress within a single system of rationality, affect wider conceptions of moral endeavor. They obscure the limitations within which moral endeavor is carried on; limitations created by moral dilemmas, limitations inherent in the situations where moral decisions are called for, or in the characters called upon to make them, not to mention the limitations created by the sheer contingency of the events which may befall men. Literature reminds us again and again of such limitations. If the philosophical theories about morality which ignore such limitations are prestigious, they themselves become agents of conceptual change in morality. In this way, philosophy becomes the darkening mirror in which moral endeavor becomes something different through ignoring limitations within which it is carried on.

Philosophical assumptions, of course, are not found simply in the work of professional philosophers. Their influence, for better or for worse, is far more widespread. If one has assumed, dogmatically, that the essence of reason is such-and-such, anything outside this essence can be dismissed. One form which such a dismissive attitude has taken in philosophy and literary criticism (not to mention politics, sociology, and anthropology) is in the ignoring of the heterogeneity of values in human life, the variety of moral perspectives. There is a constant temptation to ignore this variety and to elevate, while theorizing, those values which are one's own, and to equate them with the essence of rationality. When this is done, it then seems possible to reject perspectives of which one disapproves, not simply because they are immoral, but because they are irrational. In the fourth essay, we see how a literary critic, elevating his own moral views in the way described, can reach the conclusion that it is no longer rational, in the twentieth century, to die the kind of death that Tolstoy's Ivan Ilych dies.

The implications of such unexamined assumptions about the uniformity of the rational are explored further in the fifth essay, where the effect of philosophical prejudice in psychoanalytic thought is discussed. Here, the kind of death Ivan Ilych dies is not called irrational, but is explained in such a way as to blind us to a perspective which Tolstoy displays. Freudian assumptions may lead us to the belief that if a man, on his death bed, comes to think that he has been deceiving himself all his life, and that his life is meaningless, it must mean that he had not really wanted those things which, throughout his life, he had said he wanted. Attention to Tolstoy's *The Death of Ivan Ilych* can show us why these assumptions need to be questioned. Ivan Ilych on his death bed comes to embrace a perspective he had never known before, and it is from within this perspective that he says that he has been deceiving himself all his life. Such an admission need not entail that he had not really wanted those things which he said he wanted. To think otherwise is to obscure the possibility and importance of conversion and remorse of a certain kind in human life. The temptation to generalize and to rationalize goes deep. It can infect some of the recurring themes which have become myths and legends for us. Two of these themes are discussed in the sixth and seventh essays, namely, the stories of Oedipus and Faust. The philosophical prejudices in Freud have been so pervasive in their influence that it hardly occurs to us to question their applicability in certain contexts. To illustrate this as dramatically as possible, the question is raised in the sixth essay of whether Freud's notion of the Oedipus Complex has anything to do with Sophocles' *Oedipus Rex*. It seems unthinkable that the complex has nothing to do with the very character from whom it took its name. Yet, that is the case. Further, the unquestioning assumption that Freud's theory *must* be applicable obscures from us the perspectives on identity and fate which Sophocles wants to show us.

Premature philosophical confidence about what must be unthinkable and what must be applicable has led some philosophers to treat references to literature in philosophical discussions with disdain. They seem to think that the complexity and particularity of character and situation explored in literature are inimical to the universality and generality which should characterize any worthwhile philosophical theory. Yet, why should we think that the detail and particularity displayed in literature are options which philosophy can dispense with? Not only can ignoring such detail lead to an obscuring generality in philosophical theories about morality, but, as we have seen, it can also lead to blindness with regard to certain perspectives on human life. In the seventh essay this is brought out in the form of a tension born of a seeming paradox between philosophy and literature. Certain philosophical theories purport to tell us that "putting the future in God's hands" *must* be based on a belief that God can see the future before it occurs or on a belief that God can predict every event before it occurs. Yet, these beliefs have no obvious meaning. On the other hand, if we read Marlowe's and particularly Goethe's treatment of the Faust legend, Faust's refusal to put the future in God's hands makes a powerful impression on us. Does it follow then that what is essentially meaningless has made such an impression on us? It seems that we must embrace this conclusion if we stick to the philosophical assumptions. Here, as in the previous essays, it turns out that it is the philosophical theory which has to go. Once again, the attempt at philosophical analysis obscures perspectives which have been, and still are for some, important in human life.

Why is there such reluctance on the part of so many philosophers to acknowledge the heterogeneity of morals? Why the desire to reduce the variety of moral perspectives to a unity? To some extent, this philosophical reluctance is understandable. Irresponsible conclusions have been drawn from a recognition of the heterogeneity of morals, conclusions which philosophers may feel (wrongly) are the unavoidable logical consequences of such recognition. Because moral values do not answer to one paradigm of rationality, because some moral perspectives which were strong once are difficult to express now, it has been concluded by some that there are no objective moral values. For some, this negative conclusion became a creed in which something called the ultimate meaninglessness of life was embraced as the only certainty. In this conclusion, the glass darkens even more, and philosophical criticism of this general thesis is easy to understand. The thesis is said to be expressed in the so-called Theatre of the Absurd, and is discussed in the eighth essay in the collection. This claim cannot withstand philosophical scrutiny. In order to speak of lost, eroded, or perverted meanings, there must be some contrast with what is meaningful. Writers like Beckett do not propound any general thesis about the meaninglessness of human life, but, on the contrary, show us how some meanings have been lost and how others, of a banal kind, have a stranglehold on people's lives. These contrasts may have to be via memory of what it was possible to say and mean once but not now, or via an inarticulate longing for things to be different. In either case, no sweeping theories about the inevitable meaninglessness of life or the inherent inadequacy of language can be held to be tenable. Yet, rejecting the extremities of such conclusions should not lead us to the equally extreme alternative of denying the heterogeneity of moral opinion altogether.

At various points in these essays there is mention of lost meanings, of perspectives no longer available to us, of a darkening glass. Some critics may say that the choice of examples is significant. "The author," it might be said, "regrets the decline of various values and perspectives. The enquiry is therefore not a neutral one. All that should be said is that many people now have different values and perspectives from those which other people once held." There are many points which can be made in answer to such comments. First, even if all the examples of decline and erosion chosen were ones that I personally regretted, it would not affect one of the main philosophical issues involved, since irrespective of the presence or lack of personal regret, it is still philosophically important to give a correct account of what these values and perspectives were, and of what is involved in their decline and erosion. Nevertheless, even this much of a concession need not be made. The examples considered are chosen simply because they *do* afford instances of eroded or declining values and perspectives. There is still an essential distinction between the philosophical recognition of these possibilities and whether the philosopher can make these possibilities his own. Surely, no one would want to conflate these questions, so that one would only recognize as possibilities those which one can make one's own.

Why not say, as suggested, in face of the variety of moral perspectives, that we simply have a changing succession of points of view? The suggestion misses the complexity involved. If it were always as clear as the suggestion would have us believe, all would be well philosophically. Unfortunately, it is not so. The new perspectives often want to travel in the name of the old, claiming that the same can be achieved despite the change. Often, the new perspective cannot grasp the character of the old perspective. Of course, the same may be true vice versa.

These issues are discussed in the ninth essay in the context of an exploration of the phenomena surrounding reductionism.

The classical reductionist claims to be giving the real essence of a phenomenon by the process of reductionism. "This is what such-and-such has always been," he tells us. Pejorative descriptions of this analysis as reductionism claim that the analysis reduces the true nature of the phenomenon to something less than its original self. Yet, a third possibility exists, namely, that what reductionism expresses is not what a phenomenon has always been, but what it has become. Religious perspectives have been a major object of these tendencies. A reductionist analysis claims to show what belief in God has always been. The pejorative description of this analysis claims that belief in God has been reduced to something less than it is. Yet, what the analysis may be expressing is what belief in God has become. There is a final twist to this complex tale. The person who produces the reductionist analysis which shows what belief in God has become may be unaware of what he has achieved. Although he has shown what a belief has *become*, he may think he is showing what the belief has always been. He may be unaware that the belief could be anything other than his analysis reveals.

This possibility is discussed in the ninth essay in the context of Ingmar Bergman's work. There is no evidence that Bergman is aware that religious perspectives could have a character other than the one he portrays. Religion, in Bergman, for the most part, is a religion of compensatory consolation. Feeling rightly uneasy about this, he examines the attempt to equate God with *any* kind of love, only to find that this too fails. In fact, love itself is subjected to a reductionist analysis by which emotions become sensations and authenticity something realizable only in momentary sensory experience. If, as is suggested, Bergman shows no sign of understanding the character of religious perspectives when they were strong in people's lives, his work can become a darkening mirror in its reflection of an incomplete story as a complete one. There is no reference to a conception of religion from which a compensatory consoling religion is itself a decline. The latter is taken to be the essence of religious belief. His work darkens the possibility of our arriving at an understanding of the original perspective. Bergman, unlike

Beckett, gives no indication of the possibility that there was once something of importance which his characters can now no longer say. It is tempting to argue that if we are aware of the character of a missing meaning, we can say it again so that it can be restored. This simply does not follow. From the fact that we know how a meaningful perspective was expressed once, it does not follow that we have the ability to say it again for our own age. Memory of what was once said does not entail the ability to say it in a way which would have purchase now. In literature, the authenticity of the muted voice, so often expressed in our time, comes from a realization of this fact. In the final essay in the collection I explore this situation in the poetry of a fellow Welshman, R. S. Thomas.

Despite the poet's recognition of the impotence of his language in certain respects, he fully appreciates the need for the negative task of ensuring that in the void, a longing to say again that which was once expressed with conviction and authority should not accommodate false panaceas or pseudo-substitutes. If we are exploring a cluster of phenomena we want to describe as a darkening glass, that achievement, though the voice is muted, is not one which should be underestimated.

2/ALLEGIANCE AND CHANGE IN MORALITY:
– A Study in Contrasts

I. INTRODUCTION

IT HAS BEEN SAID that the tendency to make use of reminders drawn from literature in discussing problems in moral philosophy is not only dangerous, but needless. Dangers there certainly are, but these have little to do with the reasons offered for the needlessness of such reminders. Reminders drawn from literature, it is said, introduce an unnecessary complexity into one's philosophizing. Indeed, as Peter Winch has pointed out, according to "a fairly well-established . . . tradition in recent Anglo-Saxon moral philosophy . . . it is not merely permissible, but desirable, to take *trivial* examples. The rationale of this view is that such examples do not generate the emotion which is liable to surround more serious cases and thus enable us to look more coolly at the logical issues involved,"[1] and it carries the implication that "moral concerns can be examined quite apart from any consideration of what it is about these concerns which makes them important to us."[2]

Anyone who accepts these conclusions ignores, or fails to recognize, the tension which exists between certain ways of doing moral philosophy and the novel. I am not suggesting that this tension need exist or that it is inevitable. One is faced by the contrast between complexity and simplicity: the complexity of the novel, and the comparative simplicity of contemporary moral philosophy. The student of moral philosophy may be surprised at the suggestion that his subject is simple; he may

---

1. Peter Winch, "The Universalizability of Moral Judgments," *Ethics and Action*, pp. 154–155.
2. Ibid., p. 155.

protest that it is difficult enough. But I am not equating simplicity with easiness. What I mean by the comparative simplicity of moral philosophy is the tendency to examine human conduct within narrow boundaries which the novelist does not hesitate to transgress. My suggestion is that in this matter it is the philosophers who exhibit this tendency who are confused, and who have much to learn from the greater complexity of the novel.

I have argued elsewhere that the ethical theories dominating contemporary moral philosophy, though different in important respects, are characterized by optimism, order, and progress.[3] These characteristics make up what might be called an abstracted concept of reasonableness. In this essay I want to explore some features of this notion of reasonableness and to contrast these with moral reasons which are rooted in the ways people live and in their conceptions of what is important in life. I shall try to bring out the nature of the contrasts by reference to some novels by Edith Wharton. The contrast depends on showing how much separates examples suggested by prevailing moral philosophies from other moral possibilities. The difficulty is in showing the force of these other possibilities. Such a showing involves an ability not given to many. The novelist with such ability brings us to see possibilities which otherwise we might not recognize.[4]

II. AN ABSTRACTED CONCEPT OF REASONABLENESS

Before turning to an examination of Edith Wharton's work, more needs to be said about the notion of reasonableness I want to criticize. At first, it may seem doubtful whether different viewpoints in contemporary moral philosophy can be seen as sharing an abstracted concept of reasonableness. After all,

3. "Some Limits to Moral Endeavor," the next essay in this collection.
4. I am grateful to Mr. D. L. Sims for emphasizing this point in a discussion of this paper at the University College of Swansea English Society.

much seems to separate those who say that there is something called human good and harm by reference to which one can assess in general what people ought to do, and those who say, not only that each person must decide his ultimate moral principles for himself, but that anything could constitute such principles for a person. Yet the differences lessen when one is told that a person must not simply be free to choose his ultimate moral principles, but must also act rationally in doing so. This latter stipulation means, it is said, that the agent's principles must be such that he is prepared to abide by them himself as well as expecting other people to abide by them. Despite the fact that it is recognized that some fanatics will legislate in such a way that their principles will make them subject, in certain circumstances, to what no reasonable man would want, the general impression one receives is that there will be a large measure of agreement in men's moral principles. Because men generally want to attain and avoid the same sorts of things, their principles, it is said, framed with such consequences in view, are unlikely to show drastic divergencies. Behind this view, no less than that which makes an explicit appeal to human good and harm, is to be found the notion of what all men want, which psychologically, if not logically, tends to limit what could count as ultimate moral principles.

It is true that obstacles to the attainment of human good are recognized, but impediments, such as lack of experience and imagination, are seen as contingently related to morality. If all the facts concerning what are in people's interests were known, there would no longer be any room for disagreement about how men should conduct their lives.

Such is the philosophical neighborhood in which an abstracted concept of reasonableness can grow. One can easily imagine a character emerging from this background. We could call him the reasonable man. Of course I am not suggesting that one could ever meet such a man. But that one could not do so is precisely the point, since the caricature is constructed on confused presuppositions which are latent in a great deal of contemporary moral philosophy. As we examine six features of the reasonable man's character, those who are acquainted with recent discussions in ethics will recognize in him, though he is nameless, a familiar friend.

The first characteristic of the reasonable man is that he has reasons for his moral allegiances. He will tell you proudly that his values are not without foundations. Since these foundations, human good and harm, serve as justifications of his allegiances, the relation between the allegiance and its grounds must be contingent. It would seem to follow that his moral principles have the status of well-tested hypotheses, well-founded generalizations, or well-grounded policies. Still, this is not something about which the reasonable man would feel apologetic. On the contrary, he will point out that if one has made a mistake in one's assessment of whether allegiance to a principle is conducive to human good, it is far better to abandon or to modify the principle than to persist in one's unreasonableness. The reasonable man is always prepared to change if called upon by reason to do so.

The second characteristic of the reasonable man follows from what I have just said. The reasonable man has reasons, not only for his allegiances, but also for his changes. If moral beliefs and actions are subject to an external measure of validity, it should not be surprising if faulty assessments are made from time to time. Change, when it comes, is justified by appeal to the same criterion that justified the prior allegiance, namely what all men want to attain and what all men want to avoid, human good and harm. Change, for the reasonable man, is always reasonable change.

The third characteristic of the reasonable man is extremely important. He believes in the unity of reason; for him, reason is one. There are many different moral beliefs, but they are all either right or wrong. This is decided by bringing them all to the bar of reason. Thus, when the reasonable man changes his beliefs, he has done so by coming to a greater appreciation of the same external measure that brought him to his initial moral beliefs.

In the light of his belief in the unity of reason we can appreciate the fourth characteristic of the reasonable man, namely, that when he changes he always changes for the better. When he changes his moral beliefs he has a deeper grasp of what is and what is not reasonable, but he is still appealing to reasons of the same kind. Therefore since his change is a change within the same rational terms of reference, his change, being more reasonable than his former allegiance, is a change for the better.

Fifthly, since the reasonable man always changes for the better, the beliefs he has discarded or refused to believe in can be regarded as outmoded, outdated inhibitions, or as irrational taboos.

Finally, the reasonable man is likely to regard wider moral changes in society, when he agrees with them, in the same way as he regards his own moral changes. Society is progressing to a more rational morality; it is coming of age, casting off its old inhibitions and taboos. Those who resist the changes he agrees with will be regarded by the reasonable man as defenders of the *status quo*, as those who do not realize that we live in a real world, as being inhibited by old taboos and bound by outworn habits and customs.

No doubt additional characteristics of the reasonable man can be thought of, but I believe the six I have outlined are sufficient to illustrate one form that an abstracted concept of reasonableness can take. Adherence to such a concept obscures the essential heterogeneity of moral beliefs and the very different account of moral allegiance which is called for, once this heterogeneity is recognized. Examples play an essential role here, since in terms of the issues they present one can show, as Winch has said, that "the seriousness of such issues is not something we can add, or not, after the explanation of what those issues are, as a sort of emotional extra: it is something that 'shows itself' . . . *in* the explanation of the issues."[5] If this is right, then what is and what is not morally important cannot be determined independently of the variety of issues that present themselves. It cannot be determined in general in terms of an abstracted notion of reasonableness. In turning to the issues which are embodied in the novels of Edith Wharton, we shall

5. "The Universalizability of Moral Judgments," p. 155.

find that the notion of reasonableness we have been discussing can claim literary critics as well as philosophers among its victims.

III. ABSTRACTION, REASONABLENESS AND THE CRITICS

Edith Wharton is concerned with allegiance and change in morality but, for her, these notions are not abstractions. On the contrary, they are rooted in the New York of the last third of the nineteenth century and the early years of the twentieth century. She depicts the upper middle-class life of New York in the 1870's and 1880's as a life dominated by a hierarchical family system. Free and undisturbed by major crises, it laid great emphasis on tradition, decorum, and honesty in business. If its mannerly code was broken, one was expected to break it without scandal. The young men of the community practiced law, but in a half-hearted way which left plenty of time for frequent dinings and European excursions. Edith Wharton is alive to the force of convention in the world she depicts. Speaking of *The Age of Innocence* she says that "what was or was not 'the thing' played a part as important . . . as the inscrutable totem terrors that had ruled the destinies of (their) forefathers thousands of years ago." She describes people as living in "a kind of hieroglyphic world, where the real thing was never said or done or even thought, but only represented by a set of arbitrary signs." The easiness with which this conventionality can be appreciated has blinded critics to the moral dimension in Edith Wharton's work. Guided by very different moral beliefs, critics have abstracted selective elements from the situations and made them a picture of the whole. For example, Blake Nevius, describing old New York, says that

> The real drama is played out below the surface — the impec-
> cable, sophisticated surface — and communicates itself, if at all,
> to the observer by means of signs which only the initiate can
> read. Hence the significance, to old New York, of certain ges-
> tures by which the private drama is made public: that fright-
> ening portent of social annihilation, the "cut"; the dinner

invitation from the van der Luydens, the invitation to occupy a prominent box at the opera, or the presence of Mrs. Manson Mingott's carriage before the door, all signalizing reinstatement; the sudden flight to Europe, which is the solution to every serious emotional crisis. These were the less arbitrary signs. By and large however the acquired manners of old New York lend themselves to what Edith Wharton termed "an elaborate system of mystification."[6]

Edith Wharton herself sees far more in *The Age of Innocence*. Into the society we have described comes Countess Olenska, fleeing from a broken marriage and threatening to divorce her husband. As she is an ex-member of old New York society, the influential families decide that she must be prevented from bringing scandal on herself and on them. Newland Archer is chosen to present their case to her. He is himself betrothed to May Welland in whom many critics have seen a perfect product of the society Edith Wharton was portraying. In presenting the case, however, Newland Archer's relationship with Ellen Olenska changes. What begins in criticism, ends in love. But he has put his community's case too well. He has convinced Ellen Olenska that personal happiness is not the most important thing in life. He shows her values connected with honor, time, tradition, obedience, and sacrifice. Despite their love, they part. Archer marries May Welland, but even after her death when he has a chance to meet Ellen Olenska again, he lets the opportunity go by, convinced that nothing that could happen as a result of such a meeting would be as real as the considerations that parted them in the first place. The moral notions involved in the relationship between Newland Archer and Ellen Olenska are at the center of the story.

Why have many critics distorted these moral notions in their discussions of *The Age of Innocence*? The answer lies in the fact that having already laid down what is to count as reasonable conduct, they cannot see anything in the novel other than a straightforward tale of a weak man trapped by a trivial society, unable to take the opportunity of freedom and a life

---

6. Blake Nevius, "On *The Age of Innocence*," *Edith Wharton: A Collection of Critical Essays*, pp. 166.

worth living. There is no doubt in their minds that Newland Archer ends defeated.

Newland Archer's defeat, it is suggested, can be seen in the way meeting Ellen Olenska changed his attitude to May Welland. At first Blake Nevius tells us,

> He is the willing accomplice of a society "wholly absorbed in barricading itself against the unpleasant," and his appreciation of May Welland is based on this precarious ideal: "Nothing about his betrothed pleased him more than her resolute determination to carry to its utmost limits that ritual of ignoring the 'unpleasant' in which they had both been brought up." In the story that follows Edith Wharton tries to make clear what this innocence costs. The measure of change wrought in Archer's outlook by his experience with Ellen is suggested by a sentence occurring midway in the novel, before the echo of his earlier belief has quite died away: "Ah, no, he did not want May to have that kind of innocence, the innocence that seals the mind against imagination and the heart against experience!" ... When he returns to May Welland, it is to the ultimate realization that, like John Marcher in James's "The Beast in the Jungle," he is the man "to whom nothing was ever to happen."[7]

The evaluations involved in this criticism are fairly obvious: it is reasonable to be open to change, experiment, challenge, and novelty, and unreasonable to ignore the opportunities for these things. For similar reasons, it seems to me, Edmund Wilson describes *The Age of Innocence* as follows:

> Countess Olenska — returns to the United States to intrude upon and disturb the existence of a conservative provincial society; ... she attracts and almost captivates an intelligent man of the community who turns out, in the long run, to be unable to muster the courage to take her, and who allows her to go back to Europe.[8]

These critics ignore the moral notions involved in the relations which Edith Wharton depicts. In making the separation between Ellen Olenska and Newland Archer solely a product of weakness, Wilson is distorting the moral integrity it also

---

7. Ibid., pp. 168–169.
8. Edmund Wilson, "Justice to Edith Wharton," ibid., p. 26.

exemplifies. Blake Nevius's characterization of Newland Archer is deficient for similar reasons. In discussing them further we can see how far-reaching an influence an abstracted notion of reasonableness has had on the critics.

Wilson is wrong in thinking that Newland Archer's decision to stay in old New York is simply the result of weakness on his part. Wilson finds Newland Archer's decline after his initial protest against the old ways paralleled in Edith Wharton's later works. He claims that they "show a dismay and a shrinking before what seemed to her the social and moral chaos of an age which was battering down the old edifice that she herself had once depicted as a prison. Perhaps, after all, the old mismated couples who had stayed married in deference to the decencies were better than the new divorced who were not aware of any duties at all."[9] If Edith Wharton's view of the new is open at times to these charges, is not Wilson in danger of precisely the same deficiencies in his attitude to the old? He tends to write them off as deference to decencies, and his language implies that there is little more to be found here than sham, arid convention, and doing the done thing. When he describes Ellen Olenska's role in the novel as a narrow failure to capture one of the more intelligent of old New York's social clan, there is an unmistakable implication that if intelligence had its way, everyone would break out of the self-imposed prison they had devised for themselves. Similarly, when Nevius contrasts the protectionism, conventionalism, and conformity of May Welland with the imagination, experience, protest, and unpredictability offered by Ellen Olenska, there is little doubt as to which side he thinks exemplifies intelligence, and which exemplifies unthinking obedience, "the dull unthinking round of duties," to use the description which Lionel Trilling gives to "the morality of inertia" which he claims to find in Edith Wharton's *Ethan Frome*.[10]

Of course these critics could be right, but I am suggesting that a closer examination of Edith Wharton's best work shows that they are wrong. Furthermore, they are wrong because they

---

9. Ibid., p. 29.
10. Lionel Trilling, "The Morality of Inertia," ibid., p. 145.

are in the grip of an abstracted concept of reasonableness which here takes the form of the unwarrantable assumption that intelligence must take a specific form; one that excludes the kind of intelligence and integrity one finds in Edith Wharton's old New York. The critics are in danger of abstracting a standard of intelligence and reasonableness from the variety of such standards, and using it as a means of assessing different ways of living. Insofar as they do so, they are not dissimilar to the reasonable man I characterized earlier. His first characteristic, you will recall, was his insistence that we must have reasons for our values. In relation to Edith Wharton's *The Age of Innocence* he is likely to ask for reasons for the conformity to decorum and rigid standards, and for the ignoring of opportunities for wider experience and imagination. His answer, in our time, is almost certain to be that no good reason can be found for such conformity, and that those who become its victims, like Newland Archer, are doomed to waste their lives.

"That it has all been a waste" is not an infrequent reaction on completing a reading of *The Age of Innocence*. In making such a judgment high priority is given to the importance of satisfying genuine love, talking out difficulties in frank open discussion, making up one's own mind on moral issues, and not paying too much attention to what one's parents or one's family have to say on the matter, and the conviction that since one only has one life to live, one should not allow its course to be determined by others. It is essential to understand that it is no part of my intention in this essay to criticize these moral beliefs. Still less do I want to deny that people can or should criticize different attitudes in terms of them. What I am protesting against is the equation of these beliefs with intelligence as such, such that any beliefs which conflict with them are ruled out of court as moral possibilities. In this way, conflicting beliefs can be accused of lacking intelligence and reasonableness, and the illusion created that this conclusion has been reached by appeal to a norm which is independent of the moral beliefs involved. As a result of this illusion, the moral beliefs which are said to be inferior are almost certain to be ignored or distorted. Indeed, one may find it being denied that they are moral beliefs at all.

Such is the hold of an abstracted concept of reasonableness on the thinking of certain critics. Before considering the philosophical criticisms that can be made of such an influence, it is necessary to give an account of what such abstractions ignore in Edith Wharton's work, namely, the moral ideas which enter into the relationships she depicts; one must show that these are genuinely moral ideas. This can only be achieved by waiting on the novel.

IV. WAITING ON THE NOVEL

Can one see more than dull unthinking conformity in Newland Archer and May Welland? I believe one can, and so do other critics of the work. Louis Auchincloss says that despite Newland Archer's decision to marry May Welland and not to elope with Ellen Olenska, "there is no feeling, however, that Archer has condemned himself and the Countess to an unrewarding life of frustration."[11] Why is this so? It could hardly be the case if, as we have been told, the decision was merely the product of deference to duties due to lack of nerve. There must be something more positive about the decision. The key to this is to be found in what happens when, having mechanically put the case against her divorcing her husband, Archer finds himself in love with Ellen Olenska, and pleads with her to come away with him. She has perceived a moral reality in what to him was little more than decorum. When Ellen reminds him that he is betrothed and that she is married, he replies, "Nonsense! It's too late for that sort of thing. We've no right to lie to other people or to ourselves."[12] But Ellen Olenska is able to tell him what she has learnt from him:

> "New York simply meant peace and freedom to me: it was coming home. And I was so happy at being among my own people that everyone I met seemed kind and good, and glad to see me. But from the very beginning," she continued, "I felt that there was no one as kind as you; no one who gave me

---

11. Louis Auchincloss, "Edith Wharton and Her New Yorks," ibid., p. 38.
12. Edith Wharton, *The Age of Innocence*, p. 139.

reasons that I understood for doing what at first seemed so
hard and — unnecessary. The very good people didn't convince me; I felt they'd never be tempted. But you knew; you
understood; you had felt the world outside tugging at one
with all its golden hands — and yet you hated the things it asks
of one; you hated happiness bought by disloyalty and cruelty
and indifference. That was what I'd never known before —
and it's better than anything I've known."[13]

When Newland Archer appeals to rights, their right to happiness and the fact that May Welland has no right to ask them
to forgo it, Ellen Olenska simply replies, "Ah, you've taught
me what an ugly word that is."[14]

It is true that for some time after his marriage Ellen is seldom out of Newland Archer's thoughts. He is desperately unhappy, and, without doubt, she is unhappy too. Yet, even so,
when Archer does meet her again, it is to be told, "It was you
who made me understand that under the dullness there are
things so fine and sensitive and delicate that even those I most
cared for in my other life look cheap by comparison."[15] The
force with which Edith Wharton portrays the dullness and
conventionality in society should not obscure the sterner stuff
she also shows us. As Auchincloss says, "This is the climax of
the message: that under the thick glass of convention blooms
the fine, fragile flower of patient suffering and denial. To drop
out of society is as vulgar as to predominate; one must endure
and properly smile."[16] Sometimes, the propriety of the smile
may all but hide the moral strength beneath it. This is so in
the case of May Welland.

According to Nevius, "May Welland personifies all the eva-
sions and compromises of his (Archer's) clan, she is the 'safe'
alternative." This, it is true, is how Newland Archer thought
of his wife at many times, but it leaves out a great deal if it is
meant as a final judgment by the reader. After his wife's death,
through his son, Archer learns that there was more to his wife's
character than he had realized.

13. Ibid., pp. 139–140.
14. Ibid., p. 141.
15. Ibid., p. 192.
16. "Edith Wharton and Her New Yorks," *Edith Wharton*, p. 38.

"...you date, you see, dear old boy. But mother said..."

"Your mother?"

"Yes: the day before she died. It was when she sent for me alone—you remember? She said she knew we were safe with you and always would be, because once, when she asked you to, you'd given up the thing you most wanted."

Archer received this communication in silence...At length he said in a low voice, "She never asked me."

"No, I forgot. You never did ask each other anything, did you? And you never told each other anything. You just sat and watched each other, and guessed at what was going on underneath."[17]

Another critic, Louis Coxe, in what I regard as the finest essay in Irving Howe's collection, asks,

The total commitment of May to her world and to Newland Archer: is there nothing admirable in this? Nothing of the heroic? For I believe that if any character in this novel partakes of the heroic nature, it is indeed May Welland, she of the pink and white surface and the candid glance, whose capacity for passion and sacrifice her husband never knew.[18]

Finally, are we to assume that Archer's reflections on his life, culminating in this revelation about his wife, had no effect on him, that the truths he had unwittingly conveyed to Ellen Olenska had not come home to him? Hardly. At the end of the novel we see him with another chance to meet Ellen Olenska. He thinks, fleetingly, that even if at fifty-seven it is too late for summer dreams, it may not be too late for friendship and comradeship. In the end, however, he decides not to go up to her hotel room and remains in the park. He has sent his son ahead of him and imagines how he will be received.

"It's more real to me here than if I went up," he suddenly heard himself say; and the fear lest that last shadow of reality should lose its edge kept him rooted to his seat as the minutes succeeded each other.

He sat for a long time on the bench in the thickening dusk,

17. *Age of Innocence*, p. 283.
18. Louis O. Coxe, "What Edith Wharton Saw in Innocence," *Edith Wharton*, p. 159.

his eyes never turning from the balcony. At length a light
shone through the windows, and a moment later a manservant
came out on the balcony, drew up the awnings, and closed
the shutters.

At that, as if it had been the signal he waited for, Newland
Archer got up slowly and walked back alone to his hotel.[19]

If Archer is to think of Ellen Olenska at all now, it is in the
context of the great decision she had once made, and which
had governed most of his life. Is this a man "to whom nothing
was ever to happen"?

V. PHILOSOPHICAL CONSEQUENCES OF
WAITING ON THE NOVEL

The philosophical consequences of waiting on Edith Wharton's
novel are that the artificialities of an abstracted concept of
reasonableness are revealed. The tenets of the reasonable man
are shown to be equally artificial. In fact, all these tenets are
reversed. Let us see how this comes about.

We have seen that Newland Archer, Ellen Olenska, and
May Welland, in different ways, embody the old New York
morality Edith Wharton wanted to depict. But could we say,
as some philosophers insist we must say, that these characters
have reasons for their values? On the contrary, their values constitute their reasons. Without taking these values into account,
one cannot understand their actions or even their descriptions
of situations in which action is called for. Without the values
which enter into it, the choice facing Ellen Olenska is unintelligible. Before Archer convinces her otherwise, the satisfaction of true love and her own happiness would have been of
paramount importance to her. She would have described her
elopement with Archer as a flight to freedom. But when she
becomes aware of other values, values involving suffering,
denial, endurance, discipline, she can no longer see things in
that way. She says that her former way of looking at things is
cheap by comparison. This judgment is not arrived at however
by cashing the two attitudes into a common coinage by which

---

19. *Age of Innocence*, p. 283.

one can be demonstrated to be cheaper than the other. This is how the reasonable man would have us argue. Ellen Olenska's judgment bears no relation to such an argument. On the contrary, her judgment about her former attitude is intelligible only in terms of the new moral perspective she comes to embrace.

What has become of the claim that one must have reasons for one's values? Of course, a person can provide moral reasons for an action in specific circumstances. Ellen Olenska claimed that Newland Archer gave her such reasons without realizing it. But these are not the reasons that the reasonable man has in mind. These reasons already have a moral character, whereas he is looking for a further justification for such reasons. A natural context for such talk would be those cases where a person has hidden reasons for holding moral beliefs. A so-called allegiance to moral values may turn out to be sham, hypocrisy, pretence, or self-deception. The presence of such reasons indicates that a person has a mere external relation to the values in question.

Edith Wharton depicts an external relation to values in her portrayal of Undine Spragg in *The Custom of the Country*. Undine personifies the *nouveaux riches* who were being created by the financial empires being formed in the cities of the Midwest. She comes to threaten the placid society we find in *The Age of Innocence*. Her values at any time are essentially transient, serving the constant need for new pleasures, new conquests. Undine goes from marriage to marriage unable to share any of the genuine enthusiasms or values of her husbands, or to appreciate the traditions of the families she enters into. Her attitude can be summed up by the way she reacts to a future husband's comment on her insistence on being painted by a fashionable portrait painter. The husband remarks, "Oh, if a 'smart' portrait's all you want!" to which she replies, "I want what the others want."[20] With such an attitude she is condemned to perpetual rootlessness. Despite the fact that she ends up by marrying someone whose love of money and status is as all-consuming as her own, our last glimpse of her sees her

20. Edith Wharton, *The Custom of the Country*, p. 70.

regretting that as a result of her divorces she can never be the wife of an ambassador!

It is precisely because Undine Spragg has reasons for her values which are externally related to those values that we see in her a fundamental rootlessness in which no form of decency can grow or flourish. The difference between Undine Spragg and the characters in *The Age of Innocence* we have discussed can be expressed once again by saying that whereas she has reasons for her values, their values were their reasons.

These conclusions have drastic consequences for the reasonable man's notion of moral change. For him, since the reasons for such change must be of the same kind as those which supported prior allegiances, change occurs within a unified rational system. The inadequacy of this view can be brought out by reference to one incident in *The Age of Innocence*.

Despite the fact that Archer's son reveals depths of character in his mother which his father had never appreciated, he can hardly appreciate them. For Dallas, the son, his parents' attitudes are dated, outmoded, eccentric. Louis Coxe says, rightly, that

> For Dallas it would have been so simple: run away with Ellen Olenska and hang what people will say. . . . Times have changed, and in this simpler and freer world of Dallas' young manhood, there are no occasions to exercise the feelings nor nourish passion. . . . Can Dallas or anyone like him begin to understand the meaning of the kind of feelings Archer has known? Have they the time? the imagination? the passion? What can the notion of a buried life mean to one who can conceive only of surface?[21]

To Dallas, the relationship between his parents is "a deaf and dumb asylum."

If one compares the views of Newland Archer's generation with those of his son, can one appeal to a common criterion of reasonableness which would bring out the character of the differences between them? It is difficult to see how one could do so in general. What we see is that many of the values of one

---

21. "What Edith Wharton Saw in Innocence, *Edith Wharton*, pp. 157–158.

generation mean little to the other. With the social changes Edith Wharton describes so well, the old values of respect for tradition, endurance, loyalty, faithfulness, and the possibility of a buried life, that is, burying one's strongest desires, are eroded by the increasing dominance of new values characterized by frankness, openness, articulate honesty, courage, and experiment. A common criterion of reasonableness is not necessary in order to explain such changes. One need only bring out the content of the opposing values to show how they naturally militate against each other. To call one set of beliefs irrational often obscures what disagreement amounts to in this context; that the disagreement is itself an expression or a product of a moral judgment.

If these conclusions are correct, one can no longer believe, as the reasonable man does, in the unity of reason. Fundamental changes in moral perspectives need no longer be seen as the rejection and replacing of hypotheses or policies within a single framework within which moral beliefs must be determined. Old values do die, and new ones take their place. What separates Archer and his son is not a matter of different tentative beliefs within a common notion of reason but, rather, different ways of looking at the world, different conceptions of what is important in life.

If these differences in moral perspective are not recognized there is a danger not simply of distorting the reality of radical change, but also of misdescribing discarded beliefs as taboos and inhibitions. We see this latter danger exemplified to some extent in Dallas' mildly amused view of his parents' attitudes. With later generations, with which we are more familiar, amusement gives way to arrogance. It is assumed that earlier generations have wanted all along to be just as we are. It is often suggested that earlier generations are not really doing or believing what they think they are doing and believing. Their beliefs, it is said, form a prison which suppresses and confines their real desires.

The credibility of this view depends, to a large extent, on examples of ways of living already in decline, where nominal existence has outlived actual existence. If one thinks of lost generations, following old rules out of habit or from fear of social sanctions, alienated from their background, but unable to embrace an alternative, it is not hard to see how it can be said that these people are not at home in their world, that they are not doing what they think they are doing. In *The House of Mirth* Edith Wharton shows the empty respectability which results from the decline of old New York morality. Irving Howe describes the situation as follows:

> The action of *The House of Mirth* occurs in the first years of the twentieth century, several stages and a few decades beyond the dispossession of old New York. We barely see any representatives of the faded aristocracy; what we do see in the first half of the book are several of its distant offshoots and descendants, most of them already twisted by the vulgarity of the new bourgeoisie yet, for no very good reasons, still contemptuous of it. The standards of these characters who have any claim to the old aristocracy are not so much guides to their own conduct as strategies for the exclusion of outsiders... they have kept some pretence to social superiority, but very little right to it....[22]

In such situations as these it can be said, with justice, that things are not what they seem. What one must not do is to generalize indiscriminately from such examples. For instance, one cannot say that what Newland Archer really wants, despite what he says and does, is what his son and his generation realize. It would be distortion to say that Archer wants to follow his desires without a second thought in the way Dallas does. The notion of a buried life is important to Archer and determines the degree of importance he attaches to satisfying one's desires. To say that Archer must have been wanting all along what Dallas achieved, to say that anyone who loved the standards of old New York must have been deceiving himself, one would have to produce evidence of tension, self-deception, or alienation. When the judgment is made in the absence of such evidence, one conception of what is worthwhile in life is being made a criterion of rationality by which all other conceptions must be judged. At this stage, a moral judgment has been

22. Irving Howe, "A Reading of *The House of Mirth,*" ibid., p. 122.

changed into a metaphysical thesis about what all men want and the essence of rational conduct. No such thesis can be found in Edith Wharton. Louis Coxe says that in contrasting Newland Archer, the near-rebel, with May Welland, the total conformist,

> a lesser novelist would have been content to rest, in the mere showing of the processes by which an American with separatist tendencies is broken to harness and curb. [This corresponds to what Edmund Wilson saw in the novel.] That she does not leave it at this adds dimension to the book and to the novelist's vision. The emphasis rests finally upon the ways in which an individual, in more or less settled times, can come to identify his illusions with those of his world. The rightness or wrongness of such identification we may determine if we can, though for my part I would say that the triumph of Edith Wharton's realism strikes one as most sweeping in just her very refusal to draw any such line: she seems merely to say, that is the way things were for these people. Had you done differently, it would have been a different time, place, and cast.[23]

This brings us to the last characteristic of the reasonable man, namely his tendency to see the society to which he belongs as the product of a coming of age in which old inhibitions and taboos have been cast off. The confusion is in the claim that this *must* be the case, and in the a priori ruling out of the possibility of decline and loss in a society. There is no confusion in the claim that a whole society could be in the grip of self-deception. Edith Wharton, in writing *The House of Mirth*, asked herself how "could a society of irresponsible pleasure-seekers be said to have, on the 'old woes of the world', any deeper bearing than the people composing such a society could guess?" She answered: "A frivolous society can acquire dramatic significance only through what its frivolity destroys. Its tragic implication lies in its power of debasing people and ideals."[24] That such comments have a point is not in dispute. What is in dispute is the larger claim that the heterogeneity of morals can be reduced to some kind of rational unity.

---

23. "What Edith Wharton Saw in Innocence," ibid., p. 160.
24. Edith Wharton, *A Backward Glance*, p. 207.

When some beliefs and values give way to others, some may want to condemn the old ways as wrong, and even as wicked. That is their privilege. What cannot be said, in general, is that the old ways were irrational, that men had reasons for adopting them which seemed good at the time, that men discovered better reasons for rejecting them, and having thus progressed again and again, have now achieved the freedom which only reason can bring. Such wholesale judgments are invariably confused. What one can say often is that a society is better or worse than its predecessors in certain respects. Edith Wharton however shows us another possibility, namely, that of refraining from such judgments and being content to observe that whereas people once thought about certain matters in a particular way, we no longer do so.

I am not suggesting that the literary judgments about Edith Wharton, which, I have claimed, many critics ignore, can be arrived at independently of the moral beliefs or sympathies of the critics. To do so would be to advocate a concept of literary criticism as abstracted as the concept of reasonableness I have been attacking. A critic must be able to sympathize with a variety of moral beliefs in order to recognize their seriousness. A critic's moral beliefs may be such, however, as to rule out certain attitudes as trivial, and a novel which gave serious attention to these would be criticized by him for this very reason.[25] If this happened with too many moral beliefs, however, the critic's narrowness would itself count against his standing as a critic.[26]

VI. CONCLUSION

In the brief look we have taken at Edith Wharton's novels, we have reversed and rejected all the reasonable man's principles. If I am right in thinking that these principles underlie a great deal of contemporary moral philosophy, the reason why there

25. These points were made by Mr. H. O. Mounce in the discussion referred to in note 4.
26. I examine one example of such narrowness in "Moral Presuppositions and Literary Criticism," in this collection.

should be a tension between moral philosophy and the novel is not hard to find.

I shall end as I began by calling attention to the misgivings that are felt by some philosophers about giving a detailed analysis of examples taken from literature. In his *Critique of Linguistic Philosophy*, C. W. K. Mundle is wary of what he detects as "a method of teaching ethics (which) has become popular in parts of Wales and England. This is to read long extracts from Russian novels or Existentialist plays, describing moral dilemmas." Mundle says that "when well done, this is an excellent way of starting arguments about *what* you would have done in the problem situations. And, sometimes, about *why*."[27] To this, as we have seen, Edith Wharton would reply, "Had you done differently, it would have been a different time, place, and cast." Mundle's concern to determine the content and justification of moral conduct goes with his conception of moral philosophy as the discovery of "rules as to how *people* in *general* ought to act." After all, he argues, since all moral problems and beliefs are called "moral," we must be concerned with the same thing in all of them.

Our discussion of Edith Wharton's work should help us to see that the question of what we mean by allegiance and change in morality does not admit of a *general* answer. The assumption that moral philosophy can provide such an answer is but another symptom of the desire for tidiness and simplicity in ethics from which attention to literature can help to deliver us. As Eugene Kamenka has said, "The complexity of individuals and 'their' interests has long been recognised in literature, especially in the novel; it is time that it was more clearly recognised in ethics."[28]

---

27. C. W. K. Mundle, *A Critique of Linguistic Philosophy*, p. 14.
28. E. Kamenka, *Marxism and Ethics*, p. 35.

3/SOME LIMITS
TO MORAL ENDEAVOR

1

THE QUESTION OF THE WAYS in which moral considerations place limits on human action is one which can never be far away from central issues in moral philosophy. It is generally agreed that some account must be given of the limiting role of moral considerations, since, without one, one is left with a mere caricature of human action. That caricature would consist, roughly, of a picture of human action as the calculation of the most efficient means of attaining predetermined ends. Within this context, of course, there is legitimate talk of limits. If a man has a purpose in mind, the very character of that purpose rules certain means out of consideration. It does so, not only by showing that some means are more effective than others in securing the desired end, but also by circumscribing a certain area of relevance so that courses of action which fall outside it would not even arise for consideration. Thus, if what I want to do is to add to the money I have in the bank, various suggestions may be made to me. I may be told to leave it where it is, buy a business with it, invest it, gamble with it, or a thousand other things. People would differ over the effectiveness of the means proposed, but not anything could count as possible advice. If someone told me to give all I had away or to go for a long walk, I might take this as a way of telling me to forget the purpose I had in mind, but I could not take it as possible means of attaining that end.

Purposive activities must not be ignored in an account of human behavior. It would be foolish to do so, since it is hard to see how one can speak of human activities as rational or irrational without ever mentioning the purposes of those activities and the means which lead to them. Seeing the bearing which one thing has on another is often a matter of seeing how one thing leads to another. The point to stress, however, is that this is often, but not always, the case. This is why J. L. Stocks spoke of "the limits of purpose"; he wanted to deny that purposive action exhausted the character of human actions. Indeed, if that were all there were to tell, things would be very different from what we know them to be:

> If this were a complete account of human nature the world would be a very different place from what it actually is. If desire and its service were the whole of life there would be no fondness for places and buildings, no contemplative enjoyment of sights and sounds, no ties of affection and friendship, but only the continual grasping calculation of something to be got from men and things as they served a more or less transient need. The convenience of a utensil would be the highest form of praise.[1]

We know, however, that things are not like this; that there is such a thing as moral praise and blame; that there is a concern, not simply with working out the best ways of getting what we want, but with the character of our wants and the nature of our strivings to satisfy them. Here we have a limit placed on human action which is different in kind from the limits which our purposes place on the means we employ. The limits set by moral considerations constitute what Stocks calls "an additional principle of discrimination," since more is taken into account than our purposes and the best ways of achieving them. When purpose and its execution have said all there is to say, there remains the question of whether such a course of action can be undertaken in the name of decency.

It is very tempting to minimize the differences between the limits which purpose imposes on action and those limits determined by moral considerations. It is tempting to suggest that morality is an additional guide to human conduct which gives men, not concerns which are different in kind, but purposes which are higher on the scale of human desires, purposes which

---

1. J. L. Stocks, *Morality and Purpose*, pp. 39–40.

constitute what a man really wants in the end. In this way, morality, like any other means, would be concerned with the attainment of human purposes and with removing or minimizing any difficulties which stand in the way. I have been suggesting that this misrepresents the ways in which moral considerations place limits on human conduct. Peter Winch makes the same point in his inaugural lecture when he says that

> ... of course, men try to attain goals and they encounter obstacles in their way: lack of money, lack of various kinds of natural ability, lack of friends, opposition by other men, to name just a few. But morality has nothing much to do with helping people to overcome any of these. On the contrary, were it not for morality, they would often be a great deal easier to overcome.... Morality, we are told, is a guide which helps him round his difficulty. But were it not for morality, there would be no difficulty![2]

Moral considerations impose a limit on our purposes and their execution which the distinction between means and ends cannot account for, since means and ends alike come under moral scrutiny. Yet in passing it should be said that to say that such scrutiny imposes limits on our conduct, though correct, may mislead if talk of limits is conceived too narrowly. It may give the impression that moral considerations play a purely negative part, namely, that of preventing men from doing what they want to do and pronouncing vetoes from time to time on their plans and aspirations. While it is true that moral considerations limit our actions in this way, they also constitute a limit in another sense. To appreciate it, one must not think of the limit simply as a boundary which curtails expansion, but also as the boundary of a territory which has riches to offer to those who pass over into it which cannot be found elsewhere. If moral considerations condemn meanness, they also extol generosity; if they condemn lying, they have a regard for truthfulness. Generosity, truthfulness, kindness, loyalty, etc. are not mere negations or restrictions, but positive virtues and ideals in human life which for many make that life worth

---

2. Peter Winch, "Moral Integrity," *Ethics and Action*, p. 172.

living. Morality is as much a discovery of the worthwhile as a condemnation of the worthless.

Instead of pursuing the above point further, I want to take a brief look at some recent accounts of the relations between moral considerations and human actions. I want to suggest that if there are dangers of presenting a caricature of human action if one neglects to take account of the limits imposed on it by moral considerations, there are also dangers of caricature involved in attempting to give an account of these limits. I shall take a brief look at three accounts presented in moral philosophy.

II

According to the first account of moral values I want to consider, an account which owes much to the work of R. M. Hare,[3] such values do constitute a limit on human actions. Moral values are the product of our commendations, evaluations, and prescriptions. Men decide their ultimate moral principles and, in theory, anything could count as a moral principle. On the other hand, moral principles are also the product of reason and are therefore universalizable. Thus, we expect our moral judgments to win the assent of any reasonable man placed in similar circumstances. Granted that a fanatic could hold that one should be free to kill anyone one dislikes as long as he accords this right to anyone who wishes to kill him for the same reason, we do, nevertheless, call such a man a fanatic, and his kind make up a very small minority. Normally we find a general agreement in the things men prescribe because of an agreement in the kinds of things men want and need. Furthermore, the commendations and prescriptions which men make form a rough-and-ready hierarchy in their eyes. Moral maturity consists in recognizing this hierarchy; recognizing when one moral rule takes precedence over another; always being alive to circumstances which present exceptions to our present rules. To tell the truth blindly, without considering

---

3. See R. M. Hare, *The Language of Morals* and *Freedom and Reason.*

whether the principle applies to the given case, is the very antithesis of moral sensitivity. Thus, corresponding to a hierarchy in our purposes and methods of attainment, we have a hierarchy of commendations and prescriptions. The morally mature man not only puts aside his previous purposes when moral considerations demand that he should do so, but also puts aside some moral considerations in deference to others once he begins to appreciate the relations between moral rules and their exceptions. The discrimination of moral maturity is matched by its sincerity. The moral man's actions are as good as his word. What he believes is to be found in what he does; and failure to act in accordance with professed belief is generally a sign of insincerity.

In the second account I want to present to you, an account which owes much to the early views of Philippa Foot,[4] moral beliefs are not conceived as limits on human purposes. They cannot be so conceived since, according to this view, they constitute the best means of attaining those purposes. There are certain things which all men want, things which make up human good. Similarly there are things which all men want to avoid, things which make up human harm. Acting according to moral beliefs is the way to attain human good and to avoid human harm. A man needs the virtues in order to flourish just as a plant needs water in order to grow. Sometimes men do not realize this; they think they want other things. This is the case when men ignore moral considerations or disagree about them. Such disagreement and lack of attention are understandable, since the appreciation of what constitutes human good and harm often requires experience and imagination. Once all the facts were known, however, such shortsightedness and disagreement would be rectified, since the facts would reveal human good and harm. Since all men appeal to such facts in

---

4. See Philippa Foot, "Moral Arguments," and "Moral Beliefs," *Virtues and Vices*. For criticism of these views see D. Z. Phillips, "Does It Pay To Be Good?" *Proceedings of the Aristotelian Society*, 1964-1965, 45–60, and D. Z. Phillips and H. O. Mounce, "On Morality's Having a Point," *Philosophy* 40 (1965), 308–319. Later papers in her collection show that Philippa Foot no longer holds these views, but the views as such are still influential.

deciding what is good and bad, ideally, though often not real-ized in fact, moral values would commend themselves to all men in an agreed hierarchy of priorities.

The third account of moral beliefs I want to consider, an account which is to be found in the early views of A. I. Melden,[5] denies that alleged facts concerning human good and harm could somehow establish for us what is good and what is evil. On the contrary, it is argued, men come to have a regard for certain ways of doing things, come to extol a certain char-acter in human actions and relationships, but this concern does not depend on anything external to itself which is meant to demonstrate its validity. Furthermore, no one thing can be ac-cepted as a definition of such concern, since there is a complex of varied moral beliefs within most societies. Different institu-tions and movements are characterized by different ideals, dif-ferent rights and obligations. On many occasions, not all the rights involved can be satisfied, not all the obligations can be fulfilled. What is important, however, it is argued, is that all the moral factors involved in the situation are considered. There will always be exceptions to rules which state that certain rights should be fulfilled or that certain obligations should be met. There is no exception to the rule that rights and obliga-tions should be considered when they are involved in a situa-tion in which a moral decision is called for. Given that such consideration has taken place, the people involved will recog-nize the procedure by which a decision is reached as being characteristic of a not uncommon moral wisdom. Within an institution such as the family, for example, decisions are ac-cepted even when they do not satisfy all the rights involved. In this way, it is argued, the family is maintained as a moral com-munity. Similarly, when the claims of a man's family conflict with the claims of his work, the decision which a man makes after due consideration and which is accepted, sustains the wider moral community of which family and work form a part. In this way, within something called the total moral com-

---

5. See A. I. Melden, *Rights and Right Conduct*. This view is influen-tial, though modified by Melden in *Rights and Persons*.

munity, a hierarchy of decisions can be agreed on and progress made.

What are we to say of these three accounts of the relations which are said to hold between moral beliefs on the one hand and human purposes and methods for attaining them on the other? They represent views which, though different in ways which it would be important to bring out in other contexts, can be said to have three characteristics in common, namely — order, progress, and optimism. While they see that moral beliefs place limits on human conduct, they characterize those limits as ordered in some kind of hierarchy of importance, so that a man will know where his allegiance lies without too much difficulty.

I said at the outset that if moral considerations are left out of an account of human activities one has a mere caricature of those activities. Man is represented simply as calculating the best ways to get what he wants, whereas we know that he also cares about ideals, rights, and obligations, with all that entails. Nevertheless, it is also possible to present a caricature of men's moral concerns, and I suggest that our three accounts have come close to doing so. We are asked to accept that men aim for certain things, but that above these considerations of efficiency and attainment are moral considerations to which the former must always be subordinated. The method and order of this subordination is something which reasonable men will agree about. Purposive activities afford the opportunity for a rich moral harvest, and if the reapers are few that is only because men lack experience and imagination and are sometimes mistaken about what they really want. Once these shortcomings are removed, moral considerations, already in a system of priorities, will bring order to the range of human desires. Thus ethics and rationality are made to coincide: the moral thing to do is also the reasonable thing to do. A man learns to put first things first, not only in his purposive activities, but in his moral concerns as well. Ideally, what is important in a man's life is seen in the orderly subjection of his purposes and methods of attainment to an already ordered set of moral values. These values are brought to bear on his actions as a hierarchical system which commends itself to him as being what he really wants or as the values of a community he wants to perpetuate. If the ideal were realized in practice, a man would go about his business choosing which goals he favors, which human relationships he enters into, which decisions he makes, all in accordance with his hierarchical system of moral beliefs. The picture is one of order, progress, and optimism. It constitutes what I mean by the second caricature of human activity.

III

When we turn from these tidy philosophical accounts of the ways in which moral beliefs place limits on human actions to look at actual situations, do we not want to accuse these accounts of an oversimplification and falsification of the facts? If asked what accounts for these distortions, I think much of the answer would be found in the neglect of the sense in which I want to speak of the limits to moral endeavor. The sense I have in mind is not that in which moral considerations place limits on human actions, but that in which moral endeavor itself is often subjected to limits. The three accounts we have considered give little, if any, hint of these. On the contrary, they speak as if the subjection of human wants and desires to moral considerations were an orderly progressive procedure. But is this the case? Is there a blueprint by which a moral order, agreed on by everyone or almost everyone, is imposed on our activities? What is one to make of remorse, helplessness, the impossible good, the unanswerable difficulty, the restricted sphere of action, and countless other barriers to moral endeavor? These are what constitute the limits to moral endeavor, and when we take account of them, we begin to recognize the three outlines I have presented as attempts to account for moral considerations in human activities, but as caricatures of those activities nevertheless. This conclusion can be underlined by considering four contexts in which one would want to speak of limits to moral endeavor.

Since I have spoken elsewhere of the first limit to moral endeavor I want to mention, I shall not dwell on it for very long in this essay.[6] I refer to moral dilemmas. If one accepts the reality of such dilemmas, one can see how the optimistic progressive picture of the relations between moral considerations and human conduct becomes less plausible. When one finds oneself in situations where, whatever one does, one is going to hurt someone, talk of arranging goods in an order of priority often seems out of place. The discovery of what is morally possible for one in such situations is not the elevation of a good in an order of priority such that once the order is established one does not have to worry about the lower reaches of the scale. On the contrary, as I have argued elsewhere, even after a person has decided what he must do in these situations, he may still feel remorse for having committed the evil which his decision inevitably involved. When one lies to save a friend further suffering despite the fact that one's whole relationship with him has been characterized by absolute straightforwardness and honesty; when one has to go against the wishes of parents who have sacrificed a great deal for one in deciding to marry a certain girl or to take up a certain job; when a man is forced to kill another person in order to save a child's life; talk about establishing an order of goods would be a vulgar falsification for many people. They did what they had to do, but they did not glory in it. In the cases I have mentioned, a trust in truthfulness has been betrayed, great sacrifice has been counted an insufficient reason, a life has been taken: all these are considered to be terrible, and the decisions which brought them about and had to be taken were terrible decisions nevertheless. It is essential to recognize that in moral dilemmas, the discovery of what must be done often involves one in evil, pain, and suffering.

The above account of moral dilemmas is unacceptable to those who think that moral decisions establish or reflect an ordered hierarchical system of goods. It can be no part of the philosopher's intention to deny that there are such people, people who in one way or another can describe their activities as

---

6. See D. Z. Phillips and H. O. Mounce, *Moral Practices*, esp. ch. 8, "Moral Dilemmas." See also D. Z. Phillips and H. S. Price, "Remorse Without Repudiation," *Analysis* 28, no. 1 (1967), 18–20.

putting first things first. What can be said is that such people, from the very nature of the case, cannot be faced with dilemmas such as those I have described. For them, there are no such dilemmas. If they present philosophical accounts of moral endeavor which allow no place for these moral dilemmas, they can be accused of falsifying the facts and obscuring moral possibilities. Within the variety of moral attitudes and responses one finds the man who sees his life as the establishing of a moral order which reaches out for higher and higher achievements. One also finds the man who morally does not know where to turn, and in making his decisions hopes that he will not hurt too many people. One thanks God that he is getting better all the time: the other thanks God if he finds he is no worse. Philosophical accounts of moral endeavor must not deny the first his heights, but neither must they deny the second his limits. I have been insisting on the recognition of these limits by philosophers, and on the fact that moral decisions often carry with them measures of guilt almost equal to any good achieved.

In the moral dilemmas we have considered, the limits to moral endeavor come from the fact that not all the moral beliefs involved can be acted on. Yet, in resolving the dilemma a person discovers what he must do. In making his decision he discovers something about himself; he discovers what was possible for him. In the second context of some limits to moral endeavor I want to consider, however, there is often no difficulty in seeing what the outcome of a situation ought to be; no difficulty in appreciating what morality requires. The trouble is that all this is thwarted by the situations themselves; the situations themselves limit the possibilities of moral endeavor.

In William Faulkner's novel, *Sanctuary*, Benbow, a city lawyer, accidentally falls into the company of a group of liquor pedlars, one of whom, Popeye, is a killer. He has to spend a night in the company of these men. Later, when one of the gang is killed, Benbow has no doubt that Popeye has murdered him. The local leader of the liquor pedlars, Goodwin, is accused of the crime. Benbow feels that he must do something to help. After all, it was quite clear that Goodwin was being accused unjustly, that Popeye was going to get away with a murder, and that Goodwin's mistress and their ailing child needed his help and protection. He believes unquestioningly that he can help because he believes that justice and truth will prevail. When he fails to get Goodwin to testify against Popeye, he pursues his enquiries further until he persuades Temple, a college girl who witnessed the murder and who has since been abducted by the murderer, to give evidence. The results are disastrous. Temple gives false evidence which damns Goodwin who meets his death at the hands of an infuriated mob.

We might agree with Benbow that Goodwin was accused unjustly and that he ought to be acquitted; we might agree that Popeye was guilty and that he ought to pay for his crime; we might also agree that a false conviction would be disastrous for the accused's mistress and child. It seems to follow inevitably that something should be done about these things. But this conclusion does not follow. As we have seen, all Benbow's attempts at making things better made things infinitely worse. What Benbow lacked was psychological insight into the character of the people with whom he was dealing. He was an outsider who did not appreciate the forces and counterforces at work in the situation in which he found himself. To have psychological insight one must have a knowledge of men and the lives they lead. One must be acquainted with their different ideas of what is worthwhile in life and with how they would react to various circumstances. In short, one's knowledge must extend beyond one's immediate circles. Benbow's knowledge does not extend thus, and therefore he has no knowledge of the liquor pedlars who are social outcasts. He cannot appreciate their way of thinking, their sentiments, and their fears. Goodwin knows how useless it would be to give evidence against Popeye. As soon as he did so his days would be numbered. One way or another Popeye would claim his revenge. This is what Benbow cannot understand. His thoughts are governed by ideas of justice prevailing and the security of the law. These ideas meant little to Goodwin. He had been in jail, struggled for existence, and risked his life many times. He knows that it is better to take his chance in a trial without saying a word about

Popeye, than to ensure his own death by testifying against him. Benbow has no idea of the influence the murderer has had on the young college girl plunged into what for her was a world of nightmares.

No doubt Goodwin would have agreed with Benbow that justice, truth, and fairness are fine things, but he might well have asked, "What has that to do with the situation I find myself in?" Benbow failed to recognize the limits which the situation placed on the pursuance of his moral ideals. He was convinced that he ought to help, whereas he should have seen that there was little, if anything, he could have done to help.

I have emphasized one example in order to show that it is just as important to recognize that there are situations in which one should not try to help, as it is to recognize situations where help is called for. The conviction that one *must* help to relieve distress, and that it *must* be possible to help, is a tempting but mistaken doctrine. There are plenty of examples other than the one we have considered which illustrate this truth, but one more will suffice. A man may feel that he must try to help to keep his friend's marriage from breaking up. It might well be the case, however, that nothing can be done from the outside, that the difficulties are such that there is no solution to them. To interfere in such circumstances is usually to court disaster and to make matters worse than they were before. Once again, there may be no disagreement about the things one should strive for in marriage, or about what an ideal outcome of present difficulties would be. Nevertheless, it is recognized that, in the case in question, these things are not possible. The difficulties place limits on moral endeavor and limit the moral possibilities open to would-be helpers.

A persistent optimistic moral theorist would try to avoid the conclusions of this essay, conclusions which he would find extremely distasteful. He might suggest that the realization that nothing can be done to help in various situations is itself a moral realization. Even if this is so, however, it can in no way obscure the limits to moral endeavor which those situations illustrate. Recognizing that one can do nothing to help in certain situations may be the product of moral or psychological insight, but one could hardly call it a moral achievement. The insight in question, far from being a source of moral satisfaction, is one of the reasons for that sense of helplessness which sees that there are limits to moral endeavor, and that often the morally admirable action is simply not possible.

The third context in which some limits to moral endeavor can be found is related to the examples we have just considered. In those examples I referred to situations which limited the possibility of moral endeavor in various ways. In the examples I want to consider now, moral endeavor is limited, not by the situations in which it is called for, but by the people it is required of. We have just seen how mistaken it is to assume that in all situations where help is needed it makes sense to think of providing it; to assume that where morally satisfactory outcomes can be thought of abstractly, it must be possible to implement them in actual situations. It is equally mistaken to assume that if we can think of something morally finer and more admirable than we have attained, we should, if that description is correct, aim for those ideals. It is easy to accept that a man's attempts to be better may fail, but it is harder to see that sometimes a man should not try to be better. Yet, to recognize the third context of some limits to moral endeavor is to accept this conclusion. This can be shown by considering three examples.

A minister of religion may have no doubt that a fellow minister who works in the city slums has a deeper sense of vocation than himself. Let us assume that his judgment is correct. It certainly does not follow that he too should go to work in the slums. He knows only too well that if he did he would make a complete mess of things. He may also recognize that more often than not the question does not even arise for him: that his sense of vocation is not deep enough for such a commitment. He concludes, rightly, that it would be foolish of him to endeavor to be like his fellow minister. He accepts his limitations.

Or again, consider a married couple who start off their marriage with certain ideal conceptions of what married life ought to be like. They may know of marriages where these ideals are realized to a large extent. Very soon, however, they have to accept the fact that their marriage is not going to be like that. This does not mean that their relationship is devoid of any integrity, but it is not what they thought it might be. They conclude, rightly, that it would be foolish of them to try to emulate or seek after the kind of relationship they believe is deeper. They settle for less.

In Dostoyevsky's *A Nasty Story*, Ivan Ilyich Pralinsky is full of ideas of social reform and equality, although a sense of his own social superiority is never absent from his presentation of these ideas. One evening he discusses his views with a colleague and his superior in government service.

> "And I persist in the idea, and put it forward on every occasion, that humanity, and specifically humanity to inferiors, of the official to the clerk, the clerk to the porter, the porter to the lowest peasant — humanity, I say, may serve, so to speak, as the corner-stone of the coming reforms and generally of our regenerated society. Why? Because. Take the syllogism: I am humane, therefore I am loved. I am loved, consequently they feel confidence. They feel confidence, consequently they believe in me; they believe in me, consequently they love me . . . no, what I mean to say is that if they believe in me, they will believe in the reforms as well, they will understand, so to speak, the very essence of the matter, so to speak, they will morally embrace one another and settle the whole thing amicably and fundamentally."[7]

His colleague comments, "We shan't be able to stand it," but Ivan does not understand what he means. On leaving his host and having to walk home Ivan passes the house of one of his minor clerks whose wedding supper is taking place. The scene is one of great merriment and jollity. Ivan sees a chance of putting his love of humanity into practice. He is sure that after an initial bewilderment and surprise at his arrival he will be welcomed as an example of the reformed society to come. In this spirit he enters the wedding-feast. The results are disastrous. The guests cannot forget his official status and are extremely

---

7. Fyodor Dostoyevsky, *The Gambler/Bobock/A Nasty Story*, pp. 189–190.

uncomfortable in his presence. Champagne is brought to him although the household cannot afford it. Ivan realizes that he is ruining the occasion. Later, when the party regains its liveliness, Ivan, eating and drinking too much, can see that his intrusion has been put down to drunkeness. His plans for preaching fellowship and equality are shattered and becoming drunker and drunker he is reduced to seeking reassurances that he has not disgraced himself. In the end he is so ill that he has to be put to bed. He is given the best bed, the bridal bed. Ivan is ill for eight days. When he returns to the office he cannot face anyone. He is relieved to find that the clerk has put in for a transfer to another department. Ivan's love of humanity is replaced by very different conclusions:

> "No; severity, severity, nothing but severity!" he almost unconsciously whispered to himself, and suddenly his face was suffused with bright red. He felt ashamed and oppressed as he had never done in the most unbearable moments of his eight-day illness. "I wasn't able to stand it!" he said to himself, sinking helplessly into his chair.[8]

No doubt in Dostoyevsky's story the social situation limits the possibilities of moral endeavor as much as the limitations in Ivan's character. Nevertheless, the story does show how nasty the consequences can be sometimes when a man attempts to do what is morally beyond him or what is morally misconceived. I do not deny that others in Ivan's position might improve as a result of greater moral endeavor. The same point could be made of the other two examples I have mentioned. I am also taking for granted that self-deception is absent in these cases; that people are not appealing to assumed limitations in themselves to get out of doing what they could if only they tried. What I am insisting on is that people can come to the conclusion, rightly, that it would be foolish of them to try to be better than they are in certain respects. I am insisting that these pessimistic conclusions cannot be ruled out as signs of moral seriousness.

---

8. Ibid., pp. 237–238.

It may be argued that having given up trying to be better, people will no longer see any worth in the qualities and ideals they have failed to achieve. Cynicism may result from such failure, but it is not a necessary consequence of it. Pessimism about oneself is not incompatible with moral seriousness. This is difficult to accept if, like some moral philosophers, one holds that what a man believes to be decent is shown only in what he achieves. The unattainable good, for a serious person, is a constant comment on the little he has achieved. In the first example I considered, the minister of religion may see his fellow minister's sense of vocation as a judgment on his own. In that way, the life he admires becomes a source of humility in his own. The unattainable good, so far from being a moral irrelevance, is often, when recognized, the occasion for understanding, pity, and compassion.

In many of the examples I have considered, it makes sense to say that but for certain limitations things might have been different. A lot of distress could be avoided if people had more moral or psychological insight. Things would be different in many relationships and vocations but for the limitations of the people involved. In the fourth and final context I want to consider, however, one cannot point to a limitation of character which accounts for things going in a certain way. I have in mind situations in which we say, "They didn't stand a chance"; "Life became too difficult for them"; "Things went against them"; where our reason for saying so is not any moral defect in those whom life has made its victims. I shall simply remind you of one striking example: Hardy's *Tess of the D'Urbervilles*. There is nothing in Tess's character which shows why she should end up being executed for murder. The interest of her parents in their likely descent from the D'Urbervilles, a noble family; the fact that she is sent to claim kin to a nearby family who had simply appropriated the D'Urberville name and is seduced by Alec D'Urberville; the early death of her illegitimate child. All these are things which happen to her despite herself. Her misfortunes continue when, after her marriage to Angel Clare, he cannot forgive her for what has happened, despite the fact that she has forgiven him a worse fault. Separated from her husband who leaves the country, her path crosses that of Alec D'Urberville again. After long persistence on his part and his assurances that her husband would never return, she agrees to live with him. Her sense of the wrong which has been done to her had made her indifferent to what happens to her in the future. When, however, Angel Clare does return, ready to admit that he has wronged her deeply, it is too much for her to bear. The course of her life seems to rise before her in mockery, and in anguished torment she kills Alec D'Urberville.

We want to say that life has been too cruel to Tess; that it was too much to expect anyone to bear. We have no hesitation in giving assent to Hardy's choice of subtitle, *A Pure Woman*. The limits which life placed on Tess's endeavors occasion the following reflections by Hardy early in the novel:

> Nature does not often say 'See!' to her poor creature at a time when seeing can lead to happy doing: or reply 'Here!' to a body's cry of 'Where?' till the hide-and-seek has become an irksome, outworn game. We may wonder whether at the acme and summit of the human progress these anachronisms will be corrected by a finer intuition, a closer interaction of the social machinery than that which now jolts us round and along; but such completeness is not to be prophesied, or even conceived as possible.[9]

There is something approaching an attempt at such completeness in the three theories in contemporary moral philosophy that I outlined earlier. They present a picture of ordered moral priorities and optimism. There is little indication of "the social machinery which jolts us round and along." I have sought to correct this picture by providing reminders of some limits to moral endeavor. It may well be true that where paying attention to moral considerations is concerned, the reapers are relatively few, but it should not be assumed that a ready-made harvest awaits those who attempt to reap, that success inevitably crowns the endeavors of men of good will.

---

9. Thomas Hardy, *Tess of the D'Urbervilles*, pp. 53–54.

IV

In this essay I have mentioned four contexts in which some limits to moral endeavor can be found: moral dilemmas, situations which limit what is morally possible, limitations in character which curtail moral endeavor, and circumstances in which life's burden has become too heavy for a person to bear. What if these contexts are ignored by moral philosophers and others who may write on such subjects? The consequences may be far-reaching. By ignoring such cases the very notion of moral endeavor has new limits set on it; the concept of moral endeavor is itself changed. One might want to say that ignoring such cases brings about a decline in our conceptions of moral endeavor. Yet, even without making any moral judgment one can speak of a limiting of our conceptions. If certain ways of regarding moral problems and difficulties are constantly ignored, misunderstood, or misrepresented, those ways will sooner or later cease to be part of our conceptions of moral problems and difficulties. The contexts I have mentioned can be considered in the light of this conclusion.

If the kinds of moral dilemma I mentioned are not taken into account, people will fail to see why anyone should regard such dilemmas as tragic; why anyone should feel, even after arriving at a decision, acting on it, and not wanting to repudiate it, that he still has blood on his hands. The idea of a dilemma would gradually change to what it has already become for some, namely, a question of establishing priorities among competing claims, and of going forward with confidence and without a backward glance once that priority has been established. To continue to feel remorse in such situations, it will be said, is to be in the grip of what some psychologists have condemned as "unproductive guilt." The moral house can always be put in order.

Consider what might happen in a society where, increasingly, the limitations of character and the situations which limit moral endeavor which I have mentioned are not recognized. It is probable that the idea that there must be a solution to every difficulty would become even more prevalent than it is

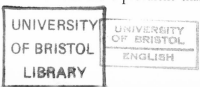

already in certain circles today. If this were to happen, the very idea of what a difficulty is would have changed in important respects. Difficulties would now be regarded as signs that something had gone wrong, in much the same way as a flaw in a product shows that there is something wrong in the techniques of production. In a society where difficulties are thought of in this way, there is also likely to be much talk of "success" in personal relationships, and many formulas offered to ensure such success. In such a context, it is not hard to see how friendship, for example, could become a commodity and the provision of it a skill. Even now a social worker can give the advice "that it is the duty of a social worker to establish a relationship of friendship with her clients; but that she must never forget that her first duty is to the policy of the agency by which she is employed."[10] It is also easy to see in such contexts how the cardinal sin would be refusal to be helped, since this would be described as pride or antisocial behavior.

Furthermore, in a society where "success" is the key word, the notion of living with insuperable difficulties is likely to decline. This is seen most clearly in changing conceptions of marriage. I deliberately emphasize extreme cases. When marriage vows are thought of as eternal and unbreakable, difficulties, when they arise, must be met in terms of them and, if needs be, lived with despite the cost. When such difficulties are regarded as things to be helped, coped with, ironed out, their persistence might well be regarded as proof that an experiment in cohabitation has failed. The vows which once were eternal may become, as they have for some, the tentative terms of reference for a trial period.[11] Similarly, if success and achievement are emphasized to the exclusion of all else, a sense of tragic inevitability such as that depicted by Hardy is likely to diminish. Life can only be too difficult, it will be said, for those who fail to take advantage of the services and help at

---

10. I owe this example to Peter Winch. See *The Idea of a Social Science*, p. 123. The quotation is from Penelope Hall, *The Social Services of Modern England* (London: Routledge & Kegan Paul, 1955).

11. Of course, I am not denying that there are a host of intermediate cases about which different things would have to be said.

hand. It is not hard to see how such ideas would have a direct effect on what people think of pity and compassion.

The changes in moral beliefs I have noted are simply some of those one would expect if the ignoring of the limits to moral endeavor, already present in our society, became more widespread. It is not the task of a philosopher to make moral judgments on such changes. It is his task, however, to take account of the variety of moral beliefs people hold, since recognition of, or failure to recognize, this variety can affect one's understanding of the nature of moral beliefs. For example, emphasizing this variety would be one way of bringing out the confusion involved in the fashionable practice of describing newly-acquired moral views as freedom from inhibition and the casting off of old taboos.

My complaint in this essay has been that the varieties of moral endeavor have not been paid enough attention in contemporary theories of ethics. These theories have attempted to be altogether too tidy and all-embracing. The character they have unwittingly portrayed is that of a moderately decent man, fairly content and at home in his world, whose achievements are solid enough if not particularly inspired. Yet, even such a man, as he goes on his orderly way, needs to recognize more than he or his philosophical creators realize at the moment, namely, how much luck, good fortune, and external circumstances need to favor him in order that he might enjoy his modicum of success. It might be argued that even where a man is favored with freedom from the kind of limits to moral endeavor we have discussed in this essay, he needs to be aware of the possibility of such limits in order to understand the endeavors of others, and in order to have a proper sense of his own. There may come a time when moral ideas are such that this will no longer be true, but such a time has not come yet. Therefore, a conceptual analysis of the relations between moral considerations and human conduct must take account of the limits to moral endeavor. This essay has tried to make a contribution to this end.

Hardy, referring to the limits which circumstances placed on Tess's moral endeavors, complains ironically that "why so often the coarse appropriates the finer ... the wrong man the woman, the wrong woman the man, many thousand years of analytical philosophy have failed to explain to our sense of order."[12] Hardy, of course, was not looking for explanations. Any sense of order which would have been satisfied with one would be defective just for that reason. It is certainly not the task of philosophy to explain away the limits to moral endeavor, but to display them in all their variety and to bring out their character. I have suggested that philosophy itself has a responsibility in doing this, since, as I have tried to show, failure to do so can itself contribute to a limiting of our understanding of moral beliefs. Philosophy often speaks of things which have a reality independent of philosophy. This is certainly true of moral philosophy. Thus, limitations within philosophy can lead to limitations in our ideas of things which are outside philosophy, not least among them being our ideas of moral endeavor.

---

12. *Tess*, p. 91.

4/MORAL PRESUPPOSITIONS AND LITERARY CRITICISM

IN THIS ESSAY I WANT TO ILLUSTRATE the importance in literary criticism of keeping apart the critic's moral opinions, the things he regards as right and wrong, good and evil, on the one hand, and the critic's opinions about morals, that is, those opinions which he regards as possible opinions, on the other. A great deal of confusion, and criticism, and lack of appreciation, can come from the equation of a critic's moral opinions with the limits of possible moral opinions.

It is clear from an article by Logan Speirs on "Tolstoy and Chekhov: *The Death of Ivan Ilych* and *A Dreary Story*," that as a critic he is dissatisfied with Tolstoy's story. Speirs claims that although "there is nothing artificial in *The Death of Ivan Ilych*, Tolstoy is desperately sincere throughout," nevertheless "there is a great emptiness in the story. It leaves the reader with a sense of sadness, of loss."[1] Why is this so? It is not entirely clear what Speirs's answer to this question amounts to. Sometimes he seems to be saying simply that Tolstoy has failed to give a convincing portrayal of Ivan's death. He mentions "a growing sense of constraints, of being on a conducted tour — a sense that we are being pushed in a pre-selected direction, that our freedom of movement is being hampered and obstructed" (p. 83). It is important to emphasize that if this criticism is justified, one would appeal to evidence in the work itself to support the assessment. The criticism is an internal one, in the sense that if the death depicted has a pre-selected character

---

1. Logan Speirs, "Tolstoy and Chekhov: *The Death of Ivan Ilych* and *A Dreary Story*," *The Oxford Review*, No. 8, 1968, 81–93, at p. 85; reprinted in *Tolstoy and Chekhov*. All references are from the journal.

about it, this is something which one would attempt to bring out by comparing the actual deathbed scene, and perhaps Ivan's conversion in particular, with what has gone before it in the story.[2] One would attempt to show that the story was forced, that its end does not seem to follow from what went before it. It is not that surprises are not allowed, but that surprises, when they come, must be such that we can readily accept them in the light of what has preceded them. Speirs's point is precisely this: Tolstoy's surprise is not a genuine surprise, it is a contrived surprise, and therefore an unacceptable one.

Speirs elaborates on his criticisms as follows:

> It is customary to decry Tolstoy for his pigheadness in hampering his creative gift in order to conduct his religious crusade. But it is important to try to establish exactly what it was that he was throwing away. We enter into Ivan Ilych's suffering — the hollowness of his life which makes his death so terrible — but we become aware that Tolstoy possesses answers, explanations which carry their own weight for him, ideas which have not been arrived at in the course of writing, but are there already, and then the element of collaboration is missing, of shared exploration. His work is no longer in the making as he writes. Tolstoy has his solutions ready. The most eagerly awaited parts arrive prefabricated. Some of the excitement of the making is missing for the artist (and this loss is passed on to the reader) — some of the mystery of discovering the unsuspected within a work which his own hands have made, of the construction as it grows, demanding fresh forms which the artist must evolve out of what is already there, the work all the time teetering precariously on the edge of noncompletion, of never being found. Now Tolstoy has stopped looking and in so doing has annihilated much potential creation. The losses are incalculable. (p. 85)

Speirs suggests that the outcome of a story must evolve in the course of writing. I do not see on what grounds this can be laid down as a necessary condition for a successful work of literature. What is one to say if an artist tells us that the end of his work was clearly in his mind almost from the outset, and

---

2. For my own account of this comparison see "Philosophizing and Reading a Story," the next essay in this collection.

that what gave him trouble was working out how to get at that point? Surely, the question of how in fact an artist worked in constructing the story is secondary to the question of whether the story when completed is successful or not. Again, what must be stressed is that judgment waits on the story. Even if it were true that Tolstoy had the end of his story in mind before he set about writing the story, the question of whether the end of the story is a satisfactory one does not depend on that fact, but on whether, given the story, we can accept its end. There is no general formula which can be applied to these matters. Only in the light of the completed work will we be able to say whether its end is satisfactory or not, and that judgment can be discussed in terms of internal evidence from the work itself.

Sometimes, in the course of his essay, Speirs makes slightly different criticisms. His new objections are not concerned with whether Tolstoy's story has prepared us sufficiently for the character of Ivan's death, but with the character of the death itself. Speirs suggests that Tolstoy achieved no more than a portrayal of self-pity. Comparing Tolstoy's short story with Chekhov's he says:

> Nikolay Stepanovitch is much more interesting than Ivan Ilych, much more of a loss at the end, in other words much less a failure than he thinks. The whole of Ivan Ilych's self-pitying reminiscences of his childhood, which precludes his regeneration, are not worth that one memory touched off when Nikolay Stepanovitch and his wife jostle each other at the bedside of their daughter. The old man means much more to us. That is his final triumph: that he commands esteem for his honesty with himself, his awareness of his own banality, his own dullness. This makes him increasingly alive, increasingly perceptive just when he thinks he is failing. He refuses easy ways out. (p. 93)

Speirs is suggesting that what we see in Tolstoy's story is not a man facing death with a certain kind of integrity, but a man desperately seeking consolation and finding it in a shallow self-pity, an easy way out. Speirs is echoing a view of Chekhov's about Tolstoy, a view which Chekhov modified later. Chekhov referred to Tolstoy as "a man afraid of death and refusing to admit it and clutching at texts and Holy Scripture." Again, whether the death of Ivan Ilych is a depiction of self-pity must be demonstrable in terms of the way in which Ivan Ilych faces his death.

At this point it might be thought that the intentions or state of mind of the artist could help to determine the appropriateness of Speirs's criticisms. Chekhov's remark could be taken in this way. Tolstoy, the man, desperately clutching at holy texts succeeds only in portraying Ivan Ilych as desperately clutching holy texts. Speirs points out that Tolstoy was facing a personal crisis at this time. He had asked in *A Confession*, "Is there any meaning in my life that the inevitable death awaiting me does not destroy?" Speirs refers to the way in which Levin is depicted at the end of *Anna Karenina*. Levin says, "My reason will still not understand why I pray, but I shall still pray, and my life, my whole life, independently of anything that may happen to me, is every moment of it no longer meaningless as it was before, but has an unquestionable meaning of goodness with which I have the power to invest it." Speirs comments, "Levin on his idyllic estate is well equipped by fortune and personality to see life so clearly. He is given the last word because Tolstoy wishes that this could be the last word" (p. 81). The suggestion is that Tolstoy's longing for a certain kind of resolution of the crisis facing him leads him to write as he does. Similarly, speaking of *The Death of Ivan Ilych*, Speirs says, "Tolstoy's desire to fill us with the fear of death is a desire to find companionship in his own fear" (p. 82).

The use Speirs makes of these suggestions is extremely puzzling. It might be interesting, for various reasons, to know Tolstoy's state of mind, or the crises he was facing, when he wrote these works, but these considerations seem quite distinct from the question of what he actually achieved in the works themselves. The question whether Tolstoy was desperately clutching at holy texts when writing *The Death of Ivan Ilych* is quite distinct from the question whether Tolstoy has actually portrayed similar desperation or something else in the work. This latter question is answered by considering the internal evidence of the work itself. Of course, someone might try to relate the author's intentions, state of mind, and achievements in the following way: Clearly, in Levin and Ivan Ilych Tolstoy intended to depict men who, in some sense or other, have come to terms with death. It may be that in fact this intention has not been fulfilled; that his portrayal of Levin's final statement amounts to no more than ignorant naivety; and that his portrayal of Ivan, despite the show of strength, cannot hide the subtle interplay of self-pity, fear, and spiritual arrogance which his death reveals. Given that the author had failed in his intentions, his state of mind at the time of writing might well form part of the explanation. One might say that Tolstoy failed to portray a man who came to terms with death because his own fear of death kept coming through in the characterization. Again, however, one could only say this if a study of the text supported such a judgment.

So far we have considered three kinds of criticism which might be made of Tolstoy's story: (a) that the course of the story does not prepare us for its outcome, that the way Ivan faces his death is forced in terms of the story; (b) that Tolstoy did not succeed in depicting what he thought he had depicted; (c) that Tolstoy's state of mind at the time of writing the story explains, to some extent, why he did not succeed in depicting what he intended to depict. If Speirs's criticisms amounted to no more than this, there would be no *philosophical* objections to them. I do not agree with the criticisms. I think Speirs is wrong about Tolstoy's story, but I have no philosophical objection to the character of the criticisms. They are criticisms which *could* be right, but which, in my opinion, are wrong. Speirs goes on to make further criticisms, however, which are different in kind. With respect to these I want to argue that the very character of the criticisms is confused. Here, it is not a question of combating criticisms which could be right, but which one holds to be mistaken, but of combating the very idea of such criticism. These further criticisms depend on an equation I mentioned at the outset, namely, the equation of a critic's moral opinions with the range of possible moral opinions.

If we look at the kind of criticisms we have already mentioned, it will be seen that an important distinction can be made in each case. First, if we say that Tolstoy's story does not prepare us for the way Ivan meets his death, we are not implying that the way in which Ivan meets his death couldn't be an appropriate outcome of any story, but simply that it is not an appropriate outcome to this story. Similarly, if we say that Tolstoy has not successfully depicted a certain attitude to death, this does not imply that there couldn't be a successful depiction of such an attitude, but simply that this depiction is unsuccessful. Again, if we say that Tolstoy's state of mind explains why he did not succeed, this does not imply that any attempt to depict Ivan's attitude to death must be connected with such a state of mind, but simply that this particular failure was so connected. In his further criticisms, however, Speirs wants to say far more than this. He wants to say that there is something inherently unsatisfactory about Ivan's attitude to death. Similarly, when Speirs says that Tolstoy gives Levin the last word in *Anna Karenina* because he wishes that it could be the last word, he means more than that Tolstoy wished that it could be the last word for himself. He wants to say, in some absolute sense, that such attitudes could not be last words, that Ivan's attitude to death could not be a possible attitude to death. In contrasting Ivan's death with that of Nikolay Stepanovitch, he says of the latter, "He refuses easy ways out" (p. 93). For Speirs, Ivan has sought an easy way out, meaning by this that such a way *must* be an easy way out, not just that it was an easy way for Ivan.

Comparing *The Death Ivan Ilych* with *Anna Karenina* Speirs says,

> *Anna Karenina* showed that there is no such thing as a last word about anything. Levin's conclusions rang true because they were given a convincing context. No general conclusion about life will ring so true again in Tolstoy's later work. Certainly one cannot imagine that the sordid end of the suburban Ivan Ilych is in fact lighted with precisely the same kind of Christian illumination that a Levin might look forward to. It is too late in the day to try to convince people that they may

sprout wings on their death-beds and this is what Tolstoy is
suddenly doing. (p. 81)

But did *Anna Karenina* show in *general* that there is no such
thing as a last word about anything? What it showed, surely,
was that there was no such thing as a last word for Anna. It
does not establish a general thesis, a truth for everyone. Because
an author depicts a situation in which it can be said, rightly,
that there is no such thing as a last word, it does not follow that
he cannot depict situations, where, for the characters involved,
there is such a thing as the last word. Yet, this is what Speirs
seems to be suggesting; he wants to turn the particular depiction
into a universal thesis.

This happens also in Speir's treatment of Chekhov's story. He
says of Nikolay Stepanovitch, the aging professor, "Now he is
conscious of approaching death, and knows that none of his
splendid, specialized knowledge, his originality within his chosen field is of use to him any longer" (p. 87). Speirs presents
this as if it were a general argument for the superiority of
Chekhov's story over Tolstoy's: one shows that there is no final
answer to death, the other tries to show that there is a final
answer; therefore, since *there is no final answer*, the former is
superior to the latter. What is the force of saying "there is no
final answer" in this way? If my argument is right it must express Logan Speirs's conviction that there is no final answer. He
is in danger of ruling out as inadmissible, however, all attitudes
to death which conflict with his own.

Chekhov's story shows how one scientific intellectual found
that the life he had lived did not sustain him in face of death.
No doubt this is to be understood, to some extent, in terms of
Nikolay Stepanovitch's relationship to his intellectual labors,
how he thought of them, what they meant to him, and so on.
But it would be ludicrous to conclude from this the general
thesis that a life dedicated to intellectual enquiry cannot sustain
a man in face of death. There are too many contrary cases to
make such a thesis even superficially plausible. For example,
although there are philosophers who disagree with Wittgenstein's philosophical opinions, few would deny his devotion to

philosophy. Norman Malcolm comments on the last days of Wittgenstein's life as follows:

> On Friday, April 27th, he took a walk in the afternoon. That night he fell violently ill. He remained conscious and when informed by the doctor that he could live only a few days, he exclaimed "Good!" Before losing consciousness he said to Mrs. Bevan (who was with him throughout the night), "Tell them I've had a wonderful life!" By "them" he undoubtedly meant his close friends. When I think of his profound pessimism, the intensity of his mental and moral suffering, the relentless way in which he drove his intellect, his need for love together with the harshness that repelled love, I am inclined to believe that his life was fiercely unhappy. Yet at the end he himself exclaimed that it had been "wonderful!" To me this seems a mysterious and strangely moving utterance.[3]

We too may find the utterance mysterious and moving, but how many would confidently rule it out of order, or try to argue that it must be something other than it seems? For Logan Speirs, Ivan's end is fear in disguise, it can never be a serious attitude to impending death. He says that "Tolstoy's insistent questions about the meaning of life are the more disturbing because the answers he foists on one with an air of triumph are impossible to accept" (p. 82). But it is essential to distinguish between a critic's inability to accept a certain attitude to death because that attitude is unacceptable in terms of a given work of literature and the a priori ruling out of such attitudes. Logan Speirs fails to keep these radically different rejections apart in his criticisms.

Let us look a little closer at the fallacies involved in Speirs's criticisms. A religious attitude to death as depicted in Ivan Ilych is certainly a final answer, a sense of certainty which, in this instance, death cannot overthrow. Clearly, Speirs does not like such attitudes. He would like to claim that they can always be explained away as disguised forms of something else. He does not try to establish this claim anywhere, and he would have an unenviable task on his hands if he tried. No doubt Speirs would think of himself as being in agreement with

---

3. Norman Malcolm, *Ludwig Wittgenstein: A Memoir*, p. 100.

Lawrence when the latter said that "morality in the novel is the trembling instability of the balance. When the novelist puts his thumb in the scale to pull down the balance to his own predilection, that is immorality. The modern novel tends to become more and more immoral as the novelist tends to press his thumb heavier and heavier in the pan."[4] Speirs would probably take himself to be in agreement also with Sartre's criticisms of Mauriac's depiction of Thérèse:

> And now here is the real reason for his failure. He once wrote that the novelist is to his own creatures what God is to His. And that explains all the oddities of his technique. He takes God's standpoint on his characters. God sees the inside and the outside, the depths of body and soul, the whole universe at once. In like manner, M. Mauriac is omniscient about everything relating to his little world. What he says about his characters is Gospel. He explains them, categorizes them and condemns them without appeal. If anyone were to ask him how he knows that Thérèse is a cautious and desperate woman he would probably reply, with great surprise, "Didn't I create her?"[5]

Sartre goes on to say that:

> In any case, the introduction of absolute truth or God's standpoint constitutes a two-fold error of technique. To begin with, it presupposes a purely contemplative narrator, withdrawn from the action ... the absolute is non-temporal. If you pitch the narrative in the absolute, the string of duration snaps, and the novel disappears before your eyes. All that remains is a dull truth, *sub specie aeternitatis*.[6]

Also, according to Sartre, it means ceasing to be a novelist, for one's characters have no freedom, no real development, no surprises, since an absolutist pattern determines everything. Hence Sartre's well-known concluding remark, "God is not an artist. Neither is M. Mauriac."[7] To some extent there is an

---

4. D.H. Lawrence, "Morality and the Novel," *Selected Literary Criticism*, p. 110.

5. Jean-Paul Sartre, *Literary and Philosophical Essays*, p. 14.

6. Ibid., p. 15.

7. Ibid., p. 23.

agreement between these remarks by Lawrence and Sartre, and what Speirs is saying. Insofar as they refer to the novelist's technique, to the way a work develops, to whether the characterization is forced, Speirs's criticisms of the end of Tolstoy's story could claim to be in the same context as the observations by Lawrence and Sartre. As we have seen, such criticisms must be justified by reference to the content and form of a particular work. The criticisms do not place undue restrictions on the possible content of works of literature. Yet, Speirs's criticisms attempt to do just that. The distinction to which I want to draw attention can be expressed as follows: from Sartre's contention that the novelist cannot take up God's standpoint and still write a successful novel, it does not follow that a man of God cannot be depicted in literature. A novelist need not take up the attitude Lawrence and Sartre are objecting to in order to characterize godly people in literature. On the contrary, for the very reason which Lawrence and Sartre mention, it is only insofar as a novelist does not do this that his depiction of religious attitudes will be satisfactory. Ironically, it is Logan Spiers who takes up an absolute God-like position in wanting to rule out such attitudes in literature. If the novelist must not play at being God, neither must the critic.

Lawrence thought the novel superior to philosophy, religion, and science because, he claimed, all three often give themselves to a misleading tidiness. He warns the novelist against importing this tidiness into his own work: "Philosophy, religion, science, they are all of them busy nailing things down, to get a stable equilibrium. . . . But the novel, no. The novel is the highest example of subtle inter-relatedness that man has discovered. Everything is true in its own time, place, circumstance, and untrue outside of its own place, time, circumstance. . . . If you try to nail anything down, in the novel, either it kills the novel, or the novel gets up and walks away with the nail."[8] What I have been arguing is that Speirs confuses the claim (false, in my view) that Tolstoy in a certain place, time, circumstance, fails to depict successfully a certain attitude to death, with the

---

8. "Morality and the Novel," p. 110.

very different claim that in no place, time, or circumstance could such an attitude be depicted successfully. He is led into this confusion by equating his own moral views about attitudes to death with what attitudes are *possible* in face of death. Strangely enough, his own moral views distort even the example from literature where he thinks these views are exemplified. Speirs says that Nikolay Stepanovitch is "increasingly alive, increasingly perceptive, just when he thinks he is failing" (p. 93). Speirs is dangerously close to saying that Stepanovitch has not failed to find an answer after all. This would be an extremely odd thing to say since Chekhov was, after all, portraying someone lost in face of death.

Speirs says of Chekhov, while comparing him with Tolstoy, "He is for his generation the more important of the two, and he knows it. He lives in the twentieth century whereas the aging Tolstoy has become imprisoned with the collapsing old order which holds him fast in spite of his anger with it" (p. 87). Speirs may be right in saying that the way in which Nikolay Stepanovitch faces his death makes more familiar reading to more people today than Tolstoy's story, but it is not at all clear what he means by saying that Chekhov's story is more important for us because of the attitude to death it depicts. In order to establish this conclusion one would have to hold that the most important thing for any generation is to have successful depictions in literature of attitudes with which it is familiar or of which it approves. It is equally important, however, to appreciate other ways of living and attitudes to life not prevalent in one's own day. Through such an appreciation one is able not simply to accord to the past the honor due to it, but also to understand better those attitudes and ways of living one finds congenial. If one regards attitudes to death, such as those of Ivan Ilych, as disguised forms of something else, or as mistakes on the way to the truth achieved by our generation, then one will be blind to certain possibilities of seriousness concerning these matters, and to the meaning of one's own judgments concerning them. If attitudes one disapproves of are thought of as "mistakes," and one's own attitudes are enshrined as "truth," one cannot grasp the kind of responsibility and commitment which moral allegiance calls for. One will be led to conclude, as Speirs comes close to doing, that an attitude which holds that there is no final answer to anything, itself transcends the context of time, place, and circumstance. He is not content to say that he cannot agree with the way Ivan Ilych meets his death. For him, it must be characterized as self-pity and condemned by his standards. It is in this way that failure to understand other attitudes to life leads to misleading accounts of one's own. It is only by realizing that notions such as "mistake" and "truth" have their meaning *within* systems of values in this context that one can appreciate what judgment and allegiance amount to here. The point is not that there should be no conflicting moral allegiances; without them, there would be no seriousness of any kind. It is rather that one's allegiance to certain attitudes should not distort the character of the allegiance of those who disagree with one. It is such a distortion, in my opinion, that one finds in Speirs's treatment of Ivan Ilych's attitude to death.

The moral values of a critic are important in attempting to understand Ivan Ilych's attitude to death, but not in the ways Logan Speirs imagines them to be important. Unless the values depicted in a work of literature mean something to a critic he will be unable to appreciate them. The critic may not agree with the values, but they must bear some relation to moral values he does hold. A critic without values, if such a person could be found, would be incapable of understanding the vast majority of works of literature. Someone may not himself share family loyalties such as those depicted by Edith Wharton in her novels, but unless loyalty were a virtue which meant something to him in other areas, he wouldn't be able to appreciate what Edith Wharton shows us about family loyalty.[9] In this way, literature can open our eyes to possibilities of moral seriousness which are wider than those we happen to agree with and wider than those prevalent in a society at any given time. Logan Speirs's attitude to his own moral views restricts his appreciation of these wider perspectives. Speirs is probably

9. See "Allegiance and Change in Morality: A Study in Contrasts," in this collection.

right in saying that "Chekhov has chosen to depict the onset of death as it is most likely to occur" if he is thinking of our time, but one cannot generalize from this particular judgment in the way Speirs is tempted to do. On the other hand, there is an important point connected with this. When Speirs says that "it is too late in the day to try to convince people that they may sprout wings on their deathbeds," he does so with an unmistakable air of superiority. His implication, no doubt, is that we have outgrown such desperate clutches at consolations. His point, if expressed differently, could have had more substance. He might have been saying that today it is getting too late to convince people that the notion of dying a good death is an important one, the notion is one which threatens to become meaningless to us. Values do not stand apart, but are related to each other in ways which form moral points of view. If such interrelated values are eroded over time, it follows that certain complex moral attitudes, certain ways of looking at things, cease to be intelligible. There may come a time when no one dies in the way Ivan Ilych died. In that event his death would be unintelligible. Could anyone die like Ivan Ilych in Huxley's *Brave New World*? I doubt it. The values Huxley depicts as dominating people's lives, utility, the intensity of transient sensations, usefulness, functionalism, when they are as pervasive as he makes them, exclude the possibility of the considerations which surround Ivan's change of attitude in face of death. I would go further: could the sensitivity to variety which, I have argued, is essential to serious literary criticism as we have known it, exist in such a society? Again, I doubt it. It must be remembered that we have this treasure too in earthen vessels, subject, like most things of value, to change, decline, and possible decay.

5 / PHILOSOPHIZING
AND READING A STORY

IT HAS BEEN SAID, with good reason, that there is a difference between philosophical doubt and practical doubt. When this is said, it is a way of emphasizing the character of philosophical puzzles and their resolution. Philosophy shows us something about things we know already; what it gives us is not additional information but an understanding of what is there to be known. The person who doubts whether he sees a man or a pillar-box in the fog has his doubts resolved when more facts become apparent. His doubts lift with the fog. But the philosopher asks whether he can be sure of what he sees when he is actually confronting a man or a pillar-box. If his doubts were practical, the philosopher should be placed in the same category as the neurotic or the madman. What the philosopher is asking, however, is not whether he sees, but what it means to say that he sees. It is the logic, not the facts, of the situation which eludes him. Because of this, we are tempted to say that his philosophical conclusions about perception do not affect what he sees. Philosophers with radically different views about perception have no difficulty in identifying colors, seeing people, or locating pillar-boxes when they wish to post a letter.

The distinction made in the above paragraph applies to other areas of philosophical inquiry. In moral philosophy, political philosophy, or aesthetics, for example, the philosopher is not concerned with making moral, political, or aesthetic judgments, but with giving an account of what it means to make such judgments. Nevertheless, one cannot conclude that the philosopher's conclusions on these matters do not affect what he appreciates about moral, political, or aesthetic matters. Although the point of philosophizing is not to have such an effect, it is undeniable that the method and conclusions of one's philosophizing often place limits on what can be understood about the mode of human discourse one is investigating. Of course, philosophical reflection may enlighten as well as obscure. We may become aware of a greater range of possibilities. In the present chapter, however, I want to show how it is possible for philosophical reflections in related fields, namely, in ethics and the philosophy of mind, to have a limiting effect in quite a different context, namely, in reading a story. The story I want to consider in some detail is Tolstoy's *The Death of Ivan Ilych*.

I. PHILOSOPHICAL PRESUPPOSITIONS

The following argument may form the philosophical presuppositions which someone brings to the reading of a story. Sometimes it seems to us that there is not a great deal of meaning in another person's life, although the person himself does not seem to recognize this. Or we may say that a person who lives for certain things is deceiving himself. But, it might be said, we must be very careful when we speak in this way. Because of arrogance and shortsightedness, we may feel that our way of life is so important and so satisfying, that we cannot see what others could possibly see in other ways of life. Shortsightedness or ignorance about the kind of people we are judging may lead us to say that they put little into their lives and get little out of them. But if we saw the people we judge as they are, and not as we had taken them to be or thought they ought to be, we might have to revise our judgments. If we paid the kind of attention to their lives that we pay to our own, we would be led to recognize a variety in people's conceptions of what is important in life.

Because of these arguments we may conclude that whether a person's life is meaningless, or whether a person is deceiving himself, must be demonstrable in terms of what that person himself says, thinks, and does. His life may be very different from our own. But although we could hardly imagine ourselves living in that way, all we can say is that such a life would be meaningless to us, not that his life is meaningless. Yet, if we reach these conclusions, how can we account for the fact that people do say that the lives of other people are meaningless when those people do not realize this, or for the fact that someone may say that an earlier period in his own life was meaningless even when he did not recognize this? These judgments seem to be ruled out if we say that it is what a person himself says or thinks which is the sole criterion of whether his life has meaning. On the other hand, we do not want to say that as long as a person says his life is meaningful it follows that it is meaningful. How, then, are these difficulties to be resolved?

Dr. Ilham Dilman has argued[1] that however these difficulties are resolved, the criteria of whether a person's life is meaningless must somehow or other be the criteria of the person whose life we are talking about. If we say that someone has not recognized that his life is meaningless, we do not reach this conclusion by applying to his life our own personal standards. Dilman argues that it does not follow "that there are not perfectly good standards for us to appeal to in judging another person's life. There are — namely, those of the other person."[2] Dilman says that "the only way to discover these is to study the person and the way he lives. But though they are personal, this does not mean that they are not objective in the sense that other people can use them as well as he. They can. It is because others can use them that it is possible for another person to point out to him what he has failed to recognize. If this were not so we could not distinguish between appearance and reality here. My point is that we do."[3] What are Dilman's general conclusions? He wants to say that if a person's life is genuinely meaningful to him, then it is, no matter what we think about it. "If, on the other hand, one suspects that it is not a meaningful life, then," Dilman argues, "whether one's suspicions are well founded or not, what one is suspecting is that it does not really mean very

---

1. See I. Dilman and D. Z. Phillips, *Sense and Delusion*, ch. 1. It is clear, of course, from Dilman's further contributions that he no longer holds this view. The view *as such*, however, is still a tempting one.

2. Ibid., p. 3.

3. Ibid., pp. 3–4.

much to the person whose life it is whether he recognizes this himself or not. If this is the case, both his life and his personality will bear marks of it."[4] On this view, if we say that a person's life has little meaning, what we are suspecting is that it does not really mean much to the person himself, whether he recognizes this himself or not. If this is the case, the person's life and personality will bear marks of it.

It must be clear that Dilman's analysis is not confused in itself. On the contrary, it may be a perfectly correct and illuminating account of many cases where we do say that a person's life is meaningless. But it is presented as more than that. It is presented as the condition of the possibility of saying that a person's life is meaningless when he himself does not recognize this; this is what is necessarily involved in making such judgments. What we have here, therefore, is a theory about judgments concerning the meaning of life, a set of philosophical presuppositions. Whenever someone in the grip of these presuppositions discovers a situation in which someone says another person's life is meaningless, though he does not recognize it, or when he hears someone say that an earlier period of his life was meaningless though he did not recognize it, he will analyze the situations in terms of Dilman's theory. I want to show how a situation of this kind is found in Tolstoy's story, *The Death of Ivan Ilych*, and how Dilman's philosophical presuppositions determine his reading of the story.

II. THE CONSEQUENCES FOR A STORY

In *The Death of Ivan Ilych* a man on his deathbed looks back over the life he has led and judges it to have been meaningless. As that life is unfolded in the story, the reader too may concur with Ivan Ilych's judgment. Dilman says that Tolstoy's story "gives a very profound portrait of a man whose life has been meaningless though he has failed to recognize this himself. It shows us what the recognition of this comes to."[5] The story concerns a man whose life in the context of government legal

---

4. Ibid., p. 4.
5. Ibid., p. 19.

appointments has been one of steady but reliable progress. Suddenly, through an accident which brings on an illness which is to prove fatal, all this is brought to an end. Confined to his bed he is given an opportunity to reflect on the life he has lived. Despite his attempts to avoid it, he comes to see that the life he has lived has been meaningless. The question Dilman is interested in is what this recognition involves.

If Ivan Ilych says *now* that his life has been meaningless, then, according to Dilman, his life could not have had much meaning for him even during the period when he did not recognize this. But in order to establish this, Dilman has to locate features of Ivan's life during the period in question to vindicate his analysis. He attempts to do so by referring to three features which he takes to be characteristic of Ivan's life. It is not really his life, Dilman argues; that is, it is not the life he would have lived had he been true to himself. He speaks of the central needs and wishes of Ivan's life as having something fake about them, and says, "What I meant was that he would not have needed to achieve a great deal of what he strived after if he had not wanted desperately to avoid facing the anguish and depression in his heart."[6] We can see how the first characteristic of Ivan's life meets the requirements of Dilman's analysis. If Ivan says his life is meaningless it must be shown to be meaningless to him even at the time he does not recognize this. This is borne out, it is suggested, by seeing how the life he leads is a screen erected by Ivan to shield himself from the anguish and depression in his heart. The second characteristic of Ivan's life which Dilman mentions is its *negative character*, by which he means "that a great deal of it is directed by the need to stave off something – fear, guilt, depression."[7] Thirdly, Dilman mentions the *destructive character* of Ivan's life, the failure to make operative that which would avoid such destruction, his inability to love or to care.

Notice that Dilman's judgment that Ivan's life is meaningless seems to ignore the nature and content of that life. What I mean is this: what makes Ivan's life meaningless for Dilman is not the

6. Ibid.
7. Ibid., p. 20.

fact that Ivan lived for the kinds of things he did live for, but the fact that these things *are used to stave off something else.* One might almost say that Dilman's basis for saying that Ivan Ilych's life was meaningless is not that way of life, but the use Ivan made of it, namely, to stave off anguish and depression. But, surely, it cannot be denied that someone could follow the same way of life as Ivan Ilych *without that life being used in the same way in which Dilman alleges Ivan Ilych used it.* Couldn't a man live for the kind of things Ivan Ilych lived for, not because he needed those things to stave off anything else, but simply because those were the things he wanted to live for? Clearly, it seems to me, the negative qualities and alienation Dilman refers to need not be present. As we have seen, according to the analysis we are considering, if a man lives the kind of life Ivan Ilych lived these characteristics *must* be present. But what sort of 'must' is this? Is it not a piece of philosophical legislation which falsifies the facts and obscures possibilities? The only reason anyone would have for saying that these characteristics must be present is that without them the prior philosophical analysis of what is involved in recognizing that a life is meaningless is shown to be inadequate. As we have seen, according to the proposed analysis, such recognition involves locating some features of the person's life *prior* to the recognition which show that he too did not see a great deal of meaning in his life even then. Furthermore, it is suggested that when a person comes to see meaning in his life, what he comes to is something he has wanted all along. What we see happening here is a philosophical theory determining our reading of the facts. What should be the case is that the facts should determine what is shown in the philosophical analysis.

I have tried to show how a particular philosophical analysis of judgments concerning the meaning of life makes it necessary for Dilman to find certain characteristics in the life of Ivan Ilych. It remains to be shown that if we come to Tolstoy's story with these presuppositions, the likelihood is that we shall misrepresent and distort the kind of life Ivan Ilych led, and the kind of recognition he attained when he came to see that life as meaningless.

III. WAITING ON THE STORY

What sort of life did Ivan Ilych lead? Tolstoy gives an indication of the features of his life in the reactions of Ivan's relatives and colleagues to his death. As far as his colleagues were concerned, "besides considerations as to the possible transfers and promotions likely to result from Ivan Ilych's death, the mere fact of the death of a near acquaintance aroused, as usual, in all who heard of it the complacent feeling, that it is he who is dead and not I."[8] Ivan shared these attitudes, attitudes which consist largely in expecting one's life to progress slowly but surely, the feeling that one has a right to expect things to go one way rather than another. Within such attitudes, there is no place for death. The end of the game is something which cannot be contemplated when the point of the game one is playing is the hope of unending progress. When Peter Ivanovich goes to sympathize with his colleague's widow, he meets another of his colleagues there who "winked at him, as if to say: ' Ivan Ilych has made a mess of things — not like you and me' " (p. 97). Ivan's widow's main interest is in finding out from Peter Ivanovich whether there is any way in which she can obtain a bigger widow's pension. These were the kinds of interests which dominated Ivan. From his youth he assimilated the so-called liberal practices of people of high station. At school, he found that what he believed to be wrong was the done thing, so he managed not to remember that these practices were wrong. More conformity follows his passing through law school and his first appointment. He has discreet affairs, the kind expected of youth. After certain legal reforms and the introduction of new judicial institutions, new men were needed, and Ivan became one of them. He is appointed an examining magistrate and so cordially terminates his old friendships. The chief attraction of his post was its power. He did not abuse this power. What was important to him was that he had it; things were within his control. He soon began to

---

8. Leo Tolstoy, *The Death of Ivan Ilych and Other Stories*, trans. Aylmer Maude (New York: Signet, 1960), p. 96. All references are from this edition.

eliminate all aspects of his life other than those connected with his work. Ivan had married a brilliant woman with good family connections and a little property. The marriage did not interfere with his work. Indeed, it enhanced his reputation. Things change, however, when his wife becomes pregnant. "He now realized that matrimony ... was not always conducive to the pleasures and amenities of life, but on the contrary often infringed both comfort and propriety, and that he must therefore entrench himself against such infringements" (p. 110). Ivan's reaction to the attentions demanded by his wife illustrate how it is his way of life which determines for Ivan what is to count as relevant and what is to count as an infringement. Ivan thoroughly enjoys the dignity, pomp, and power involved in his office. All this was as it should be for Ivan: his life "continued to flow as he considered it should do — pleasantly and properly" (pp. 111-112). Ivan's life is not one of driving ambition, but it is one in which he expects a certain order, a steady progress of events.

Suddenly, Ivan finds that he has been passed over for promotion to a certain post. He is plunged into deep depression and all his relationships are soured by his disappointment. His irritation with his employers is obvious, and this leads to his being passed over for further appointments. Now according to Dilman, Ivan's way of life can be explained as a screen erected by him to hide from himself the anguish and depression in his heart. But the foregoing shows that the very reverse is true! We can only understand the character of Ivan's depression in terms of the life he is living. If we say with Dilman that it is Ilych's depression which explains his way of life, how do we explain his depression? That seems to remain an unresolved mystery. What needs to be recognized is that his anguish and depression *are the product, not the explanation,* of Ivan's life. They can be seen as the product of Ivan's egocentricity and desire for compensation. By Ivan's egocentricity and desire for compensation I mean his tendency to see the importance of all issues as determined by their relation to himself, to think that he has a right to expect his life to go in one direction rather than another, to think that his fortunes and misfortunes are the only real fortunes and misfortunes, that his own life exhausts the meaning of reality. Ivan's egocentricity and need for compensation are illustrated by his reaction to his being passed over for promotion: "Ivan Ilych felt himself abandoned by everyone" (p. 113). They are shown in the contrast between the way in which *he* regards the event, and the way it appears to other people: "what was for him the greatest and most cruel injustice appeared to others a quite ordinary occurrence" (p. 112). Ultimately, however, the views of other people about his misfortune are unreal and irrelevant to him. Ivan Ilych thought that "he alone knew ... his position was far from normal" (p. 113). Normality, for Ivan Ilych, is understood in terms of his egocentricity and need for compensation: what is normal is that things should go well for him; what is not normal is that he should suffer any setbacks. Simone Weil has shown that this kind of egocentricity and need involves the illusion that the past has given us some rights over the future. What she says illustrates perfectly the kind of view of life Ivan Ilych possessed. She refers to the feeling that we have a right to a certain permanence: "When we have enjoyed something for a long time, we think that it is ours, and that we are entitled to expect fate to let us go on enjoying."[9] Ivan Ilych certainly feels that he has a right to expect his life to continue along a course of steady progress. When that progress is halted by a setback, in Ivan Ilych's eyes, things are not what they *ought* to be. Ivan goes to Petersburg with the sole intention of getting a job with a salary of 5,000 rubles "and be in a ministry other than that in which they had failed to appreciate him" (p. 113). His leaving, in his eyes, would be a punishment on the ministry. This is another instance of his egocentricity. Luckily, because of a shuffling of personnel he is promoted in his former ministry and is given a salary which places him two stages above his former colleagues. "All his ill humour towards his former enemies and the whole department vanished, and Ivan Ilych was completely happy" (p. 114). But Ivan did not

9. Simone Weil, "Concerning the 'Our Father'," *Waiting on God*, p. 173.

regard the change in his fortunes as a piece of luck, but as a restoration of normality, a return to the way things *should* be: "after a stumble, his life was regaining its due and natural character of pleasant lightheartedness and decorum" (p. 114). His greatest pleasure was playing bridge: "After a game of bridge, especially if he had won a little (to win a large sum was unpleasant), Ivan Ilych went to bed in specially good humour" (p. 119).

Ivan Ilych's life is not to resume its former course, however. While demonstrating to an upholsterer how he wanted the hangings draped in his new house, he slips on the stepladder and knocks his side. He takes little notice of the matter at the time, but the pain in his side becomes more frequent and severe. He cannot get any satisfactory answer from his doctor regarding the severity of his illness. His wife's attitude is that the illness is his own fault, and that he will get over it if only he'll follow the doctor's instructions. For his wife, everything is a matter of planning. Of course, her attitude is but a reflection of Ivan's own. It is important to note that the first crack in Ivan's attitude is brought about by an *accident*, by a contingency, by something which cannot be planned. According to Dilman's account, the illness simply occasions the opportunity for reflection. What I am suggesting is that Tolstoy's depiction of how the illness occurred is meant to be a contrast to, and an indication of, the kind of attitude to life Ivan had prior to the illness. For Ivan, his illness is not part of how things should be. This is illustrated, in the early days of his illness, by his irritation at any little thing which was out of place, such as a stain on the table. Later, he is faced by the unavoidability of death. He does not know what to make of it. His only consolation is that everyone's turn will come. He cannot cope with the thought of his own death because up to this point he has thought only of other people's deaths as events in his life. He has treated their deaths as signs that they have messed things up; precisely the same attitude which Schwartz and Peter Ivanovich were to take of his death. But as his *own* death approaches, he sees that he cannot view it in that way.

He sees that "death is not an event in life: we do not live to experience death."[10]

> The syllogism he had learnt from Kiezewetter's Logic: "Caius is a man, men are mortal, therefore Caius is mortal" had always seemed to him correct as applied to Caius, but certainly not as applied to himself. That Caius — man in the abstract — was mortal, was perfectly correct, but he was not Caius, not an abstract man, but a creature quite, quite separate from all others. He had been little Vanya, with a mamma and a papa, with Mitya and Volodya, with the toys, a coachman and a nurse, afterwards with Katenka and with all the joys, griefs, and delights of childhood, boyhood, and youth. What did Caius know of the smell of that striped leather ball Vanya had been so fond of? Had Caius kissed his mother's hand like that, and did the silk of her dress rustle so for Caius? Had he rioted like that at school when the pastry was bad? Had Caius been in love like that? Could Caius preside at a session as he did? "Caius really was mortal, and it was right for him to die; but for me, little Vanya, Ivan Ilych, with all my thoughts and emotions, it's altogether a different matter. It cannot be that I ought to die. That would be too terrible."

Such was his feeling.

> "If I had to die like Caius I should have known it was so. An inner voice would have told me so, but there was nothing of the sort in me and I and all my friends felt that our case was quite different from that of Caius. And now here it is!" he said to himself. "It can't be. It's impossible! But here it is. How is this? How is one to understand it?" (pp. 131-132)

Ivan's inability to cope is a direct result of the desire for permanence and control which I mentioned earlier. The view of life which involves such inability has been described penetratingly by Simone Weil.

> Our personality is entirely dependent on external circumstances which have unlimited power to crush it. But we would rather die than admit this. From our point of view the equilibrium of the world is a combination of circumstances so or-

---

10. Ludwig Wittgenstein, *Tractatus Logico-Philosophicus*, 6.4311.

dered that our personality remains intact and seems to belong to us. All the circumstances of the past which have wounded our personality appear to us to be disturbances of balance which should infallibly be made up for one day or another by phenomena having a contrary effect. We live on the expectations of these compensations. The near approach of death is horrible chiefly because it forces the knowledge upon us that these compensations will never come.[11]

When we come to consider Ivan Ilych's reaction to the recognition of the reality of death, there may seem much to commend Dilman's philosophical account of how Ivan's life prior to the recognition should be regarded. I shall try to show, however, that the passages which might be cited to support Dilman's analysis do not in fact support it, but rather, underline its inadequacies.

The first thing Ivan did, Tolstoy tells us, was to try "to get back into the former current of thoughts that had once screened the thought of death from him" (p. 132). Tolstoy's way of expressing this fact may have misled Dilman. Dilman takes the above to mean that Ivan used his way of life to screen from himself the thought of death. What I am saying, for reasons I have elaborated, is that *it is the life he leads which screens the thought of death from Ivan;* because it was the kind of life it was it made it impossible for the participants in it to have anything but superficial attitudes towards death.

To try to save himself from his newfound sense of hopelessness "Ivan Ilych looked for consolations — new screens" (p. 133). Again, this fact in no way supports Dilman's analysis. This search for screens is something Ivan indulges in *after* his recognition of the inevitability of death. It can only be understood in terms of his fear of death. One can in no way infer from this present activity the fact that Ivan's whole life in the past has been used as a screen by him. The search for consolations is an attempt to disguise the horror of death. But the search for screens fails: "*It* penetrated them and nothing could veil *It*" (p. 133). Ivan is tormented by the deception which grips everyone around him. No one will see his death for what

---

11. Simone Weil, "Concerning the 'Our Father'," p. 174.

it is. They keep treating it as a barrier to be surmounted. It is the lives they lead, the kind of life Ivan used to lead, which makes it impossible for them to entertain thoughts about the finality of death.

When Ivan says that he would like to live as he lived before, he suddenly realizes that this is not true. The things which mattered to him then now seem utterly empty. "It is as if I had been going downhill while I imagined I was going up. And that is really what it was. I was going up in public opinion, but to the same extent life was ebbing away from me. And now it is all done and there is only death" (p. 148). Ivan is forced to recognize that he has not lived as he ought to live. Tolstoy's description of what this recognition involves may again seem to support Dilman's analysis: "It occurred to him that what had appeared perfectly impossible before, namely that he had not spent his life as he should have done, might after all be true. It occurred to him that his scarcely perceptible attempts to struggle against what was considered good by the most highly placed people, those scarcely noticeable impulses which he had immediately suppressed, might have been the real thing, and all the rest false" (p. 152). This is the strongest evidence Dilman could appeal to in the story, but I do not think it yields his conclusions. The point is not that Ivan's life was a way of concealing these things from himself, or of shielding himself from them. On the contrary, he suppresses these things because they constitute threats at the time to what he really wants – the satisfaction of his need for compensation. What Ivan was brought to see during the night is *something new*, something which reflecting on death has revealed to him. "In the morning when he saw first his footman, then his wife, then his daughter, and then the doctor, their every word and movement confirmed to him the awful truth that had been revealed to him during the night. In them he saw himself – all that for which he had lived – and saw clearly that it was not real at all, but a terrible and huge deception which had hidden both life and death" (p. 152). As a result of his reflections on death, Ivan passes an unconditional judgment on his former life and calls it meaningless.

Having made this judgment, however, Ivan still does not see how the past can be rectified. His present plight seems pointless. He cannot find any explanations: " 'There is no explanation! Agony, death . . . What for?' " (p. 151). What Ivan comes to see is that it is confused, though natural, to look for such explanations. He might have echoed Simone Weil's remark, "If I thought that God sent me suffering by an act of his will and for my good, I should think that I was something, and I should miss the chief use of suffering which is to teach me that I am nothing. It is therefore essential to avoid all such thoughts, but it is necessary to love God through the suffering."[12] The way in which something similar is to be revealed to Ivan has been hinted at by Tolstoy at different times in the story. At the outset, when we are shown the different reactions to Ivan's death, only Ivan's servant Gerasim is unafraid of death. When Peter Ivanovich says that Ivan's death is a sad affair, Gerasim replies, " 'It's God's will. We shall all come to it some day' " (p. 103). Gerasim sees in death a truth for everyone, while Ivan and his colleagues saw at best a truth about Caius, man in the abstract, but one which certainly did not apply to themselves. Again, during Ivan's illness, when those around him will not recognize the possibility of his dying, Gerasim stands out as the exception: "Gerasim alone did not lie; everything showed that he alone understood the facts of the case and did not consider it necessary to disguise them, but simply felt sorry for his emaciated and enfeebled master. Once when Ivan Ilych was sending him away he even said straight out: 'We shall all of us die, so why should I grudge a little trouble?' " (p. 138). Tolstoy puts what he regards as the true attitude towards death in the mouth of a servant, in the mouth of the man who serves, who cares for others. Understanding comes to Ivan Ilych too when he is able to care for others, when he ceases to be the center of his world, when he is freed from his egocentricity and need for compensation. It happens in this way just before his death:

Just then his schoolboy son had crept softly in and gone up to

12. Simone Weil, *Gravity and Grace*, p. 101.

the bedside. The dying man was still screaming desperately and waving his arms. His hand fell on the boy's head, and the boy caught it, passed it to his lips, and began to cry.

At that very moment Ivan Ilych fell through and caught sight of the light, and it was revealed to him that though his life had not been what it should have been, this could still be rectified. He asked himself, "What is the right thing?" and grew still, listening. Then he felt that someone was kissing his hand. He opened his eyes, looked at his son, and felt sorry for him. His wife came up to him and he glanced at her. She was gazing at him open-mouthed, with undried tears on her nose and cheek and a despairing look on her face. He felt sorry for her too.

"Yes, I am making them wretched," he thought. "They are sorry, but it will be better for them when I die." He wished to say this but had not the strength to utter it. "Besides, why speak? I must act," he thought. With a look at his wife he indicated his son and said: "Take him away... sorry for him ...sorry for you too..." He tried to add, "forgive me," but said "forgo" and waved his hand, knowing that He whose understanding mattered would understand.

And suddenly it grew clear to him that what had been oppressing him and would not leave him was all dropping away at once from two sides, from ten sides, and from all sides. He was sorry for them, he must act so as not to hurt them: release them and free himself from these sufferings. "How good and how simple!" he thought. (p. 155)

Ivan no longer thinks of himself. He no longer wants to know why his life has gone this way rather than any other. He sees the senselessness of such questions:

"And the pain?" he asked himself. "What has become of it? Where are you, pain?"

He turned his attention to it.

"Yes, here it is. Well, what of it? Let the pain be." (p. 155)

Ivan is also able to say that death has been conquered. As long as he was in grip of the need for compensation, death dominated, since such an attitude could not say anything in face of it. But Ivan overcomes death in making something other than himself the object of his energy and attention. To fear death, for Ivan, is to fear the destruction of oneself, but since caring for others for him involved dying to the self, death itself lost its sting.

> "It is finished!" said someone near him.
> He heard these words and repeated them in his soul.
> "Death is finished," he said to himself. "It is no more!"
> He drew in a breath, stopped in the midst of a sigh, stretched out, and died. (p. 156)

IV. PHILOSOPHICAL CONSEQUENCES OF WAITING ON THE STORY

I have taken a good deal of time over the discussion of Tolstoy's story. There is no other way, I believe, of grasping the nature of the understanding Ivan attained on his deathbed. That understanding is obscured by Dilman's philosophical presuppositions concerning judgments about the meaning of life. According to those presuppositions, if a man says that his life has been meaningless, or if we make a similar judgment about him, we must be able to show that during the period of the life in question, his life did not really mean much to the person concerned. By waiting on Tolstoy's story we see that these assumptions can be challenged as *general truths*. The story calls to our attention one use of judgments about the meaning of life in which they are unconditional judgments of value. The life is condemned as meaningless simply because of the kind of life it is. There is no suggestion that before the judgment can be made by a person or by someone about him, it must be possible to show that the person himself did not really see much meaning in his life even before he comes to recognize it to be meaningless. None of the characteristics implied by Dilman's philosophical theory need be present. This is the case, I have tried to show, in Tolstoy's *The Death of Ivan Ilych*.

I have said that moral judgments of meaninglessness are unconditional judgments: they do not wait on what the unjust man wants or happens to think worthwhile. *Despite* what he wants or thinks worthwhile, his life can be said to be meaningless. Moral judgments intrude into, and constitute a veto on, purposes however magnificent and means taken to attain them however economic. J. L. Stocks expressed the matter well when he said,

> The moral attitude is essentially a concern for the rightness of action. A true instinct exhibits it as interfering with the execution of purpose in stigmatising as immoral the doctrine that the end justifies the means. The phrase implies that morality requires that all means shall be justified in some other way and by some other standard than their value for this or any end; that however magnificent is the prospect opened out by the proposed course of action, and however incontestable the power of the means chosen to bring this prospect nearer, there is still always another question to be asked: not a question whether in achieving this you will not perhaps diminish your chances of achieving something still more important; but a question of another kind. 'There is a decency required', as Browning said; and this demand of decency is prepared to sacrifice, in the given case, any purpose whatever.[13]

Ivan's realization of the meaninglessness of his life on his death-bed would not have the force it does were it not for the fact that it involves an unconditional judgment of value. Ivan does not deny that he had thought his life was meaningful. Now, however, he says that given the limits of that life, from a certain moral and religious perspective, it cannot be seen as other than meaningless. The philosophical theory and presuppositions we considered earlier do not allow for the possibility of such a judgment. This being so, the application of this theory and these presuppositions to situations where such judgments play a part is bound to distort these situations. This is true, as I have tried to show, of Tolstoy's story. Ivan, in the light of his reflections on death, sees his past life as meaningless simply because of the kind of life it was. Furthermore, when he comes to love and care for others, we need not conclude that this is something he has known or wanted all along. His remorse would not have revealed such a terrible pattern had he wanted it all along. What he has to face is that he had wanted other things all too much. What he comes to on his deathbed is some-

---

13. J. L. Stocks, *Morality and Purpose*, p. 77.

thing which dawns on him in the way I have tried to indicate. To think otherwise would be too rob Ivan's new understanding of the status Tolstoy ascribes to it — the status of a revelation.

6/WHAT THE COMPLEX DID TO OEDIPUS

WHY CALL A COMPLEX an Oedipus complex? It would seem perverse to do so if in fact the complex had nothing to do with Oedipus. Growing up as we do in an environment which has been influenced by Freud, one in which people who have never read a word of Freud readily explain their own and other people's behavior by reference to a complex they exhibit, perhaps our reactions go no further than this uncritical assumption. Indeed, they are not likely to go so far. Freud has brought off a takeover and the old firm is soon forgotten: "You mean there was a play? I thought Freud discovered the Oedipus complex." But even if proprietary rights are reestablished, we are simply back where we started. Freud would not have called the complex an Oedipus complex if it had nothing to do with Sophocles' play. What was implicit in the literary form, its latent if not its manifest content, is demonstrated by Freud, given a clinical analysis.

But is this so? How ironic it would be if one person who does not suffer from an Oedipus complex is Oedipus himself. Yet, that is to be my contention. The man who was unaware of Sophocles' achievement was right after all — the complex does belong to Freud, or, at least, if the Oedipus complex is latent in some works of art, Sophocles' *Oedipus Rex* is not one of them.

The perversity of this claim for Freudians is one which non-Freudians may find hard to appreciate. It is like suggesting that there are human constitutions which differ from others in not having hearts! What, no heart! The idea is unthinkable, since a heart, given its function, is central to what we mean by a human constitution. Similarly, for Freudians, the idea of a human life without the characteristic desires of infantile sexuality is unthinkable. The desires are an essential part of what we mean by a childhood. Every male child has harbored unconscious desires to kill his father and sleep with his mother. For Freudians, that is simply a fact. For Freudians, to argue that such a fact is absent in Oedipus is not grotesque simply on the grounds that these desires are shown so clearly at work in the play, true though that is, but on the grounds that the fact being disputed is one that does not *happen* to be true of Oedipus, since it is true of all men, part of human nature.

The universality of the Freudian claim does not imply a universal neurosis. This is because most of us work through the desires of infantile sexuality in the course of normal development. It is only in cases where this development is impaired that neuroses may develop in adult life. But whether the desire to kill one's father and sleep with one's mother is accommodated or not, the occurrence of such desires, we are told, is beyond dispute. This claim is a piece of a priori legislation, since given its own terms of reference it is undemonstrable. In the case of the neurotic male adult there would be no problem, given the correctness of Freud's analysis. The neurosis would simply be explained in terms of the Oedipus complex. But what of the majority who are said to have come to terms with their unconscious desires in the course of normal development? The presence of neuroses cannot be the clue to the occurrence of such desires, since in these cases there are no neuroses. The child cannot be asked to recall such desires, since in the vast majority of cases the desires are supposed to be unconscious. That leaves witnesses as our only hope. To attribute an unconscious desire to kill or to sleep with someone to a person, there must be something in his behaviour to occasion or justify such an attribution. Since in the case of many, if not most, male children, those who have witnessed their childhood can produce no such evidence, the unconscious desires cannot be attributed to them. If, despite these facts, one continues to assert that all male children have harbored unconscious desires to sleep with their mothers and to kill their fathers, the thesis does become a piece of a priori legislation. The thesis is not arbitrary, the power of sexuality and family relationships makes it foolish to say that, but it is a priori nevertheless.

The universality of the Freudian claim helps the devotee to negotiate what would otherwise be a difficulty — the absence of explicit evidence in a work of literature for the desires Freud speaks of. Despite the fact that Sophocles does not tell us or show us that Oedipus harbored unconscious desires to kill his father and to sleep with his mother, we can bring that to the play, where Oedipus is already a man, since such knowledge is the inheritance of all men, being a necessary feature of their childhood. It is true, of course, that we can take a lot for granted in the sense which works of literature have for us. The works are about human beings and their dealings with each other. This being so, everything does not have to be stated explicitly. For example, we do not have to be told that people have parents, grow up, age, and die. These things we take for granted. Nevertheless, the fact that we can take such things for granted makes a difference to the specific events which befall the characters. The events befall human beings. Yet, taking such general facts of nature for granted is very different from taking specific events of a specialized nature for granted. We can take for granted that everyone has a father and mother, but we cannot take for granted that all male children want to kill their fathers and sleep with their mothers.

Because Freudians do take such desires in human beings for granted, the essentialist presupposition may obscure other possibilities of meaning from them. That is what happens in the case of Sophocles' *Oedipus*. On the Freudian view, the play shows a man actually doing what he had unconsciously longed to do as a child. In his clinical work Freud had to come to terms with the fact that in most cases no murders or seductions had actually taken place during childhood. They occurred in the fantasies of the child. With so-called primitive savages, Freud thought it was otherwise. Lacking sophistication, there is unlikely to be a gap between desire and action in their case. Freud believed that in the beginning was the deed, a murder of the patriarchal father by the sons who envied his sexual prerogatives. He thought that this act cast light on the origins of morality and religion. He shocked many by his suggestion that this origin lay in complicity in a common murder. With a developing sophistication, the savage is repressed. What was once done is now harbored unconsciously. The horror of the Oedipus story is that the savage reasserts itself. What was harbored unconsciously is done once again. Oedipus does kill his father and sleep with his mother. He has to face the fact that he has always wanted to do this, and so inflicts a terrible punishment upon himself. Such, in its essentials, is the Freudian reading of Sophocles' play, a reading which makes it appropriate to name the complex in question, the Oedipus complex.

It is no part of my purpose to deny that there could be a story of which this Freudian analysis would be a faithful rendering. Neither is it part of my purpose to deny that were this the case, the story would be a terrible one, revealing dark recesses of the human soul. What I do deny is that this is what is revealed by Sophocles' *Oedipus*. If Freud is wrong, however, what are we to make of Sophocles' play? I suggest that we can look for an answer in terms of two notions: identity[1] and fate.

Oedipus is intensely concerned with the question of his own identity. On the one hand, he cannot accept the possibility that he, of all people, is cursed among men. Yet, when he discovers the full horror of what he has done, he cannot pretend that his identity is unaffected by this discovery. But what is it that he discovers? According to the Freudian reaction to the play, he discovers that he has actually fulfilled his unconscious desires. What Sophocles shows us is something different. He shows us a man who kills his father and sleeps with his mother *without* any such desire to do so. Sophocles' Oedipus is not a man who does what he had wanted to do, unconsciously, all along, but a man who does the last thing he would have wanted to do, the very thing which makes him cursed among men. The distinction is a vital one, since it affects what it is that

---

1. I am grateful to my colleague Mr. D. L. Sims for a suggestion concerning the importance of identity in this context.

Oedipus has to face. No doubt it is terrible to discover that one has had dark unconscious longings, but it is at least arguable that it is more terrible to discover that one has actually done, without realizing it, what one would never want to do, namely, some of the most terrible things imaginable. It also affects the reader's reaction to his fate. We may pity a man who does what he has wanted to do in the secret of his heart, if he is in the grip of a longing for the terrible, but our pity is surely different for a man who finds he has done terrible things he would never have done had he known what he was doing.

Some may react by feeling that Oedipus' remorse is irrational. How can a man blame himself for actions which he knew nothing about and which he certainly did not intend, consciously or unconsciously? Such bewilderment ignores the fact that for Oedipus the horror he discovers concerns something he has *done*.[2] His identity is inseparable from his actions. This is what Sophocles wants to emphasize. Once a man severs the connection between identity and action, the notions of identity and responsibility are changed drastically. If one were making a moral judgment, one might say that these notions are impoverished irredeemably. That much is illustrated by the work of those contemporary sociologists who seek liberation for the individual in terms of role theory. Once we realize that what were once regarded as necessities can be seen as roles, we see that we can change our roles at will. If we do not like the implications of a role, we can reject the role. Such an analysis, however, does not produce liberation, but alienation and uprootedness. It is not surprising to find that the self which such analyses produce is the naked self of modernity, outside all roles and institutions. The man who belongs to nothing feels responsible for nothing. Sophocles understood this. His Oedipus *cannot* put aside what he has done. On the contrary, his identity cannot be separated from the fact that he has killed his father and slept with his mother.

But what of the part played by fate in Oedipus? How are we to understand the words of the Chorus which talk of the in-

---

2. Cf. Peter Winch, "Moral Integrity," *Ethics and Action*, pp. 184–185.

evitable, and seem to foretell how it will all end? It is not easy for us to make sense of the Chorus. If we take its words as indicating that Oedipus' fate has been fixed by powers beyond human control, the whole matter is trivialized. Contingency is eradicated from the story and with it its tragic dimension. On the other hand, if, in an effort to preserve contingency and rid the situation of an undesirable determinacy, we treat the Chorus as merely predicting the outcome for Oedipus, again something seems to be lost. Oedipus is trying to escape something to which no sense can be given if the Chorus are no more than skillful predictors.

We have already seen that Oedipus thought that the possibility that he, of all people, was the cursed among men, was unthinkable. He had created his own fortune and status, or so he thought. Sophocles is showing us that human life cannot be thought of as entirely subject to the will in this way. There is also fate, or the acts of the gods. These intrude into the best of human plans. So it was with Oedipus, and this is what he was brought to recognize. Of course, in real life, we cannot predict the dealings of fate, or share the knowledge of the gods. By their very nature, such dealings and knowledge are not ours to possess. Nevertheless, our conception of them serves as a via negativa, it prevents men from thinking that life is entirely within their control, from thinking that reality owes them anything, or from the illusion that what is possessed must, of necessity, endure. But Sophocles wants to do more than this. He wants to show us the contrast between reality and illusion, between the knowledge of the gods and hubris. To do so we must be shown the secrets of fate, the knowledge of the gods. These are formalized and expressed in the voices of the Chorus. They express the course a life is taking with a judgment of its end, and they do so by offering a vision of a completed life, a realized fate, as a backcloth to events as they unfold. They become a commentary on the futility of ignoring the gods or fate. Thus Oedipus's tragedy is heightened as we are able to assess his own view of what is happening against the background of the revelations of the Chorus. In the end, when all is made known to him, Oedipus has to accept that he too is dependent on powers greater than himself, and that life must be lived in this recognition.

Freud changes the necessity of fate into the necessity of human desires. Freud found the reference to fate an irrational encumberance. In letters to Wilhelm Fliess he says that "the gripping power of *Oedipus Rex*, in spite of all the rational objections to the inexorable fate that the story presupposes, becomes intelligible, and one can understand why later fate dramas were such failures. Our feelings rise against any arbitrary, individual fate . . . but the Greek myth seizes on a compulsion which everyone recognizes because he has felt traces of it in himself. Every member of the audience was once a budding Oedipus in phantasy, and this dream-fulfillment played out in reality causes everyone to recoil in horror, with the full measure of repression which separates his infantile from his present state." The fact that Sophocles had no conscious intention of portraying the Oedipus complex would not have worried Freud: "The idea has passed through my head that the same thing may lie at the root of Hamlet. I am not thinking of Shakespeare's conscious intentions, but supposing rather that he was impelled to write it by a real event because his own unconscious understood that of his hero."[3] The inevitability of the will of the gods becomes the inevitability of working out the implications of infantile sexuality. What Sophocles wants to show cannot survive the change. In fact, as we have seen, the Freudian analysis obscures what is in the play. In order to see this, however, one must put aside Freud's essentialist assumptions about sexuality, fathers, mothers, and children. Only then can we appreciate how much has been lost in failing to see other possibilities of meaning. Only then can we appreciate what the complex has done to Oedipus.

---

3. Sigmund Freud, *The Origins of Psycho-Analysis*, pp. 223–224.

7 / KNOWLEDGE, PATIENCE, AND FAUST

THERE COULD BE LITTLE UNDERSTANDING of the Faust legend without a consideration of what it means to be ready or unready to commit the future into God's hands. No doubt many other themes are also involved, but this one, clearly, is central. The appreciation of the theme for many versed in contemporary philosophy may pose a problem, if not a paradox. Reading various versions of the Faust legend, they may have the impression that something important, something powerful, is being said. On the other hand, attempts to make this impression articulate may end in failure. What is more, philosophy may contribute to this failure. Philosophers have been critical of efforts to say what is meant by the phrase "the future is in God's hands." This is because, given assumptions concerning what the phrase *must* mean, it seems that the phrase is simply a product of conceptual confusion. And so the paradox is created for the philosophical reader: on reading Faust he has the impression that something important is being said, but any articulation of this impression inherits the philosophical label of conceptual confusion. Clearly, this paradoxical situation is unsatisfactory. Something has to change: either the impression that something important is being said is mistaken, or the philosophical parameters within which one is asked to articulate the impression are too narrow. In relation to the Faust legend I want to argue that the latter is the case.

Marlowe's *Doctor Faustus* ends with the words of the Chorus:

> Cut is the branch that might have grown full straight,
> And burned is Apollo's laurel bough,

That sometime grew within this learned man.
Faustus is gone: regard his hellish fall,
Whose fiendful fortune may exhort the wise
Only to wonder at unlawful things,
Whose deepness doth entice such forward wits,
To practise more than heavenly power permits.[1]

These words have to do with the fate of a man who tried to do what only God can do, a man who refused to leave to God what ought to be left to him. But how are these words to be understood? What do they amount to? Suppose we ask why a man should be prepared to put his future in God's hands, what do these words amount to? Philosophers have suggested that this question could be answered in one of two ways: either "the future is in God's hands" means that God sees the future before it occurs, or it means that God successfully predicts the future before it occurs. The trouble is that neither answer will stand up to philosophical examination. Both answers are riddled with conceptual confusion. But then we are faced with the paradox I have already alluded to: treatments of the Faust legend which depict a man's refusal to place his future in God's hands seem to be treatments of something which makes no sense anyway. The way out of the paradox is to look again at the philosophical assumptions concerning what it *must* mean to place the future in God's hands. Let us not say that this is what readiness to trust God *must* mean. Let us rather turn to the works of literature to see what it means there. Instead of approaching the works forearmed with philosophical requirements in the form of definitions of meaning (theories of thought), let us wait on the works of literature. In other words, let us obey Wittgenstein's command, "Don't think. Look!"[2] If we do this we may find that what the work of literature shows forces us to give up restrictive philosophical categories. We may then say of the treatments of the Faust theme what Lawrence said of philosophy and the novel: "Philosophy, religion, science, they are all of them busy nailing things down, to get a stable equilibrium

---

1. Christopher Marlowe, *Complete Poems and Plays*, (London: Dent, 1976). All references are from this edition.
2. Ludwig Wittgenstein, *Philosophical Investigations*, I, 66.

... But the novel, no ... If you try to nail anything down, in the novel, either it kills the novel, or the novel gets up and walks away with the nail."[3]

In this essay I want to examine two philosophical attempts to nail down, given what "the future is in God's hands" would have to mean, the fact that the phrase is meaningless. I also examine how attention to Marlowe's and Goethe's treatment of Faust shows us the way in which these works get up and walk away with these philosophical nails. We walk away in a direction which brings new vistas to our attention, vistas which some philosophers, free from the assumptions I have mentioned, have commented on. I suggest that a clearer understanding of the phrase "the future is in God's hands" would be found if we turned to Kierkegaard's treatment of the notion of patience.

Before turning to look at the two philosophical assumptions concerning what it would have to mean to say that the future is in God's hands, I do not want to give the impression that because these assumptions are confused there is no point in reflecting on them. One must work through the puzzle; one cannot simply ignore it. Also, in the course of these reflections logical light may be thrown on such notions as "the future" and "prediction." My point, however, is that such discussions are more valuable for the light they throw on these notions, than for any light they throw on what is meant by saying that the future is in God's hands.

I

Let us now turn to look at the two assumptions about what saying the future is in God's hands would have to mean. The first of these says that this means that God sees the future before it occurs. But this assumption is confused. What is the reasoning which leads to this confusion? It goes like this: Suppose it is true that I shall die when I am sixty-four years of age. It follows that the proposition "D. Z. Phillips will die at sixty-four," although it refers to an event which has not oc-

---

3. D. H. Lawrence, "Morality and the Novel," *Selected Literary Criticism*, p. 110.

curred yet, is true now, at this very moment. The thought that
the proposition is true now can lead someone to feel that since
that truth must refer to something, that something, namely,
the future, must, in some sense, exist already. "The future lies
before us" we say. It seems as if it is simply waiting to unfold
itself. Certain images may influence us when we speak in this
way. We may think of a human life as a reel of film. The
present is the flickering image on the screen. It is there for a
moment only, not made to last, essentially transient. On the one
side there is the used film which once had its day on the
screen. On the other side there is the film which is yet to appear. Yet, although the film has yet to appear, its content is
already determined. Again we may speak of human life as a
story which unfolds according to a script. There are the pages
which we have already turned. There are the pages being acted
out at the moment. Finally, there are the pages still to come.
The play has not proceeded that far yet, but we may feel that
the script is already written.

The first thing that should strike us about this thesis is its un-
checkability. We have no way of checking the content of the
film before it unfolds. This is where the analogy with the reel
of film or the script breaks down. In the case of the reel or the
script we can distinguish between what ought to happen and
what in fact does happen. Intrusions may occur which make
the director of the film shout out, "Hey! That's not in the
script." But if something happens in life, then it happens. It
may be unexpected, surprising, out of character, but it cannot
be denied. We have nothing here corresponding to the independent check on the film or play.

Someone might react by saying that although man has no
knowledge of the plan or script, God does. Life unfolds according to God's providential plan. Once again, however, the
practical consequences of this assumption are negligible. As we
have seen, there is no question of any kind of check on what
happens which would determine whether or not it is in accordance with the plan. "Whatever happens according to God's
plan" tells one very little, since if this is true *whatever* happens,
one wonders, in this context, what additional information or

insight reference to God's plan secures which one does not have already in the empty observation, "Whatever happens happens." One might well react to the further reference to God's plan in terms borrowed from Marlowe's Faustus:

> What doctrine call you this? *Che sera, sera.*
> What will be, shall be. Divinity, adieu!
>
> [1.1.47-48.]

Yet, having noted the disanalogy between human life and a reel of film or a play's script, we still have not got at the root of the temptation to think that if a proposition about a future event is true now, that future event, in some sense, already exists. One powerful source of the temptation is to think of knowing or predicting the future as a kind of seeing.[4] The fortuneteller looks into her crystal ball to see the future. Using our imaginations we may say, "I can see her face now when I tell her the news." Of course, we often do know future events before they occur. I may know what horse will win tomorrow's race. I know that the sun will rise tomorrow. I may know how a friend will react when I give him certain news — and so on for thousands of instances. But what I am doing here is not seeing, in some special way, events before they occur, but predicting on the basis of other things that they will occur. Such predictions do not entail the postulation of a realm, "the future," which I am seeing prior to its becoming the present. The mistake comes from thinking that knowing is like seeing, for once we say that to know the future is to see the future, it is almost inevitable that we shall hypostatize, make substantial, that future which we claim to know. In this way we are led to embrace the analogy of the future as the unseen film or unacted script; a film or a script which, nevertheless, some people have the power to have a preview of, and which God, since he is the author of them, has known all along.

But, now, what if we avoid the pitfalls we have mentioned by turning to the second view of what is meant by saying that the future is in God's hands, in which saying our futures are in God's hands means, not that God sees our futures before they

---

4. I am grateful to my colleague H.O. Mounce for this suggestion.

occur, but simply that his knowledge is such that he is able to predict everything that will occur? One misgiving many have felt about the idea that the future already exists in some sense or other is that it seems to leave no room for human freedom. But knowledge of the future as prediction gets around that difficulty. Some have suggested that it is helpful to think of divine foreknowledge in relation to human behavior by analogy with the relation between a master chess player and a novice. The master may know the other's play so well, and know so much about chess, that he is able to predict every move he makes. Yet, the possibility of such prediction by the master in no way implies that the novice did not make his move freely. The master simply knows what move the novice will freely make. Thus, God, whose knowledge is incomparably greater than that of the chess master, knows every move we'll make. Such divine foreknowledge does not impair human freedom in any way. To say that our futures are in God's hands simply means that God knows every move we are going to make.

I find this argument suspect. The trouble with the analogy with the chess example is that there the prediction takes place within certain well-defined limits. Similarly, we know what prediction means where horse racing is concerned. It is tempting to argue that, if all the factors were known, I could be as certain about the winner of tomorrow's 3:30 as I am that the sun will rise. Since God knows all the factors about everything, there is no future event which he does not know about. The trouble is, however, that I do not know what it means in many instances to talk of knowing all the factors such that prediction would be possible. And if a question of meaningfulness is involved, an assertion is not made meaningful simply by associating it with God.

Someone might be tempted to argue as follows. Since we can have explanations *after* events occur, why should we not say that if all the factors involved were known we could have predicted the occurrence of such events? Let us consider an example:

A child riding his toy motor-car strays on to an unguarded

railway crossing near his house and a wheel of his car gets stuck down the side of one of the rails. An express train is due to pass with the signals in its favour and a curve in the track makes it impossible for the driver to stop his train in time to avoid any obstruction he might encounter on the crossing. The mother coming out of the house to look for her child sees him on the crossing and hears the train approaching. She runs forward shouting and waving. The little boy remains seated in his car looking downward, engrossed in the task of pedalling it free. The brakes of the train are applied and it comes to rest a few feet from the child.[5]

Now, this event having occurred, also has an explanation. It goes like this:

The driver had fainted, for a reason that had nothing to do with the presence of the child on the line, and the brakes were applied automatically as his hand ceased to exert pressure on the control lever. He fainted on this particular afternoon because his blood pressure had risen after an exceptionally heavy lunch during which he had quarrelled with a colleague, and the change in blood pressure caused a clot of blood to be dislodged and circulate. He fainted at the time when he did on the afternoon in question because this was the time at which the coagulation in his blood stream reached the brain.[6]

Professor Holland points out that although there are scientific elements involved, the explanation as a whole cannot be called scientific, although the explanation is natural enough. He calls it a historical explanation of how the train came to stop. The considerations involved are, as he points out, various:

They include medical factors, for instance, and had these constituted the whole extent of the matter the explanation could have been called scientific. But as it is, the medical considerations, though obviously important, are only one aspect of a complex story, alongside other considerations of a practical and social kind; and in addition there is a reference to mechanical considerations. All of these enter into the explanation of,

5. R. F. Holland, "The Miraculous," *Religion and Understanding*, p. 155.
6. Ibid., pp. 155–156.

or story behind the stopping of the train.[7]

As Professor Holland points out, there is also a comparable explanation, also complex, of why the child was on the track at that place and time. "So now" it might be asked, "why couldn't the saving of the child be predicted if all the factors were known?" The trouble with this is that it trades on talk with which we are familiar, talk in which the factors make up what we might loosely call a system or context within which we know what it means to speak of prediction. In the present example it is true that we have two sets of natural explanation: an explanation of why the train stopped and an explanation of the presence of the child on the track. But, as Professor Holland says,

> These two explanations or histories are independent of each other. They are about as discontinuous as the history of the loom is from the history of the Ming dynasty. The spacio-temporal coincidence, I mean the fact that the child was on the line at the time when the train approached and the train stopped a few feet short of the place where he was, is exactly what I have just called it, a coincidence — something which a chronicle of events can merely record, like the fact that the Ming dynasty was in power at the same time as the house of Lancaster.[8]

If someone says that this coincidence is predictable he must provide some wider framework within which the two sets of explanations can be fruitfully correlated. I have no idea how one would even make a start on such a project.

There may be two reactions to this conclusion. One is to say that our present state of ignorance should not lead us to say that such predictions are in principle impossible. My reaction is to say that until the term 'in principle' can be given more flesh than this I do not know what it means either to agree or disagree with the assertion. The other reaction is to say that although human beings cannot say what such correlations could be between these sets of explanations such that predic-

---

7. Ibid., p. 156.
8. Ibid.

tions of such events could be made before they occur, God's knowledge is wholly different from our own and so we are unable to conclude that he could not predict such events. Again, my reaction is loss of interest. If God's knowledge and predictions are *wholly* different from ours then it is hard to see what we can know about them or how they are supposed to enter human life, what significance they can have for us.

Yet, the idea that the future is in God's hands is a thought which does impinge on human life. Against the background of such a thought certain opposite tendencies can be placed in a certain perspective: Prometheus or, our special concern, Faust. So far I have been arguing that the belief that the future is in God's hands will involve the believer in insuperable difficulties if he takes it to mean either that God sees the future before it occurs or that God can predict every future event. Still, all that is negative. We still have to give an account of the belief that the future is in God's hands. What can be made of it? And if Faust's refusal can be seen partly as a refusal to say that the future is in God's hands, what can be made of that?

Perhaps we can make some headway if we return to Professor Holland's example. He tells us that the child's mother regards the saving of her child's life as a miracle. Furthermore, she does so even after finding out all in the way of explanations which has been referred to. Why should this coincidence be seen as a miracle; or, rather, how is it possible for someone to so regard it? Professor Holland replies that

> unlike the coincidence between the rise of the Ming dynasty and the arrival of the dynasty of Lancaster, the coincidence of the child's presence on the line with the arrival and then the stopping of the train is impressive, significant; not because it is very unusual for trains to be halted in the way this one was, but because the life of a child was imperilled and then, against expectation, preserved. The significance of some coincidences as opposed to others arises from their relation to human needs and hopes and fears, their effects for good or ill upon our lives. So we speak of our luck (fortune, fate, etc.). And the kind of thing that, outside religion, we call luck is in religious parlance the grace of God or a miracle of God. But

while the reference here is the same, the meaning is different. The meaning is different in that whatever happens by God's grace or by a miracle is something for which God is thanked or thankable, something which has been or could have been prayed for, something which can be regarded with awe and be taken as a sign or made the subject of a vow (e.g. to go on a pilgrimage), all of which can only take place against the background of a religious tradition. Whereas what happens by a stroke of luck is something in regard to which one just seizes one's opportunity or feels glad about or feels relieved about, something for which one may thank one's lucky stars. To say that one thanks one's lucky stars is simply to express one's relief or to emphasize the intensity of the relief: if it signifies anything more than this it signifies a superstition (cf. touching wood).[9]

Notice that the religious and secular responses here do not depend on disputes over the natural explanations. These are admitted. The difference in the responses is seen in the ways in which the coincidence impinges on human life. Before such a coincidence some breathe a sigh of relief, while others kneel. It is in a similar way that we ought to try to see what may be involved in a religious view of life as a whole, seeing the whole of life as a gift of grace or a miracle of God. Seeing what is involved here may help us to see how Faust can be seen as the antithesis of such an attitude; how Faust's pact is not with God, but with the Devil.

We all know the story of the lady who said to Carlyle, "I've decided to accept the universe," to which he replied, "Madam, you'd better." Perhaps Carlyle's reply had a point where the lady in question was concerned, but perhaps he too misses something. The point of Carlyle's reply is to show that where the universe is concerned, there is no question of deciding to accept or not to accept. We are part of it no matter what we say. Carlyle's rejoinder is connected with a view which many philosophers have held, namely, that voluntary choice and in-

---

9. Ibid., pp. 156–157. I do not know whether Professor Holland would concede that at other times referring to the stars in their courses has meant more without being superstitious, for example, when the stars themselves are understood under a religious aspect.

evitability are mutually exclusive. You can only make a choice where there are options open to you. What can it possibly mean to speaking of choosing when one is faced with inevitabilities? Yet, despite the strength of this philosophical tradition, it is mistaken. That life is a mixture of necessities and contingencies is not a matter of choice. That is how life is, and it is difficult to imagine anything we would call a human life where this was not the case. So this is not a matter of choice. Nevertheless, despite the fact that it is not a matter of choice, there still remains the question of what sense can be made of it. Even in the midst of necessity there is still a question of will, a question of the way in which these necessities are taken up into one's life. One way in which this may be done, and which has considerable importance in religion, is what is meant by *patience*. I have suggested that it is by examining the notion of patience that we shall come to a better understanding of what is meant by saying that the future is in God's hands.

The nature of patience can be illustrated in relation to extreme suffering. At first patience seems to be a concept riddled with paradox. Kierkegaard brings out why this is so. Can one will suffering? "Is not suffering something that one must be forced into against his will? If a man can be free of it, can he then will it, and if he is bound to it, can he be said to will it? ... Yes, for many men it is almost an impossibility for them to unite freedom and suffering in the same thought."[10] Again, Kierkegaard asks, "Can anyone but one who is free of suffering, say, 'Put me in chains, I am not afraid'? Can even a prisoner say, 'Of my own free will I accept my imprisonment' – the very imprisonment which is already his condition? Here again the opinion of most men is that such a thing is impossible, and that therefore the condition of the sufferer is one of sighing despondency. But what then is patience?"[11] Kierkegaard's reply is that patience is "the courage which voluntarily accepts unavoidable suffering."[12] In this respect, he argues, patience performs a greater miracle than other forms of courage. Courage,

---

10. Kierkegaard, *Purity of Heart*, p. 172.
11. Ibid., p. 173.
12. Ibid.

normally understood, is the readiness to face an evil which could be avoided. Patience, on the other hand, is the readiness to face evil which cannot be avoided. People will say of the man who can exercise patience that he is making a virtue out of necessity. They say this disparagingly. But, Kierkegaard argues, if they really understood him, they would see that this is exactly what he does: make a virtue out of necessity. Patience is that virtue, namely, refusing to be deflected from what is good or worthwhile by the unavoidable evils and restrictions of life, and not thinking that the worthwhile is rendered worthless because of them. Patience in religion takes the form of the ability to thank, to find things worthwhile, despite the way things go. To see that the way things go is in God's hands, not in the objectionable senses discussed earlier, is to see that grace, the gift of thanks and gratitude, may transcend unavoidable evils and limitations.

Impatience, in the sense of lack of patience as here understood, is the failure or refusal to accept the unavoidable. Sometimes, as in Prometheus, this may take heroic forms. It may be a protest against sham and deception; a protest against attempts to describe evils which are avoidable as the unavoidable will of God. Yet, even where the evils and restrictions are unavoidable, there may still be a Promethean protest – a protest against a life such as this.

Yet, not all forms of impatience are heroic. Some are nothing more than a lack of the kind of virtue Kierkegaard is talking about; a refusal to accept the unavoidable in life; a desire to transcend restrictions in an act of possession and conquest. To illustrate this lack of patience we turn, not to Prometheus, but to Faust.

If someone were to ask what man has to be patient about, there is no general answer to this question. What will ask for patience in one life may not occur in another. Of course, some things can be named which all men are faced with: aging and death, for example. But what patience consists in cannot be answered in detail in isolation from the human life one is talking about. The same will be true of lack of patience. Turning to the Faust we find depicted by Marlowe and by Goethe in the first part of his work, I shall concentrate on examples of lack of patience in three contexts to be found there: intellectual enquiry, love, and morality. My argument is that it is no accident that as things lose sense for Faust patience is cursed more than anything else. Here is Goethe's Faust:

> Curse on the fragrance of the grape,
> Curse be on love's sweet festival,
> And cursed be hope, and faith, her ape,
> And cursed be patience most of all.
>
> [Faust's Study (iii), p. 84][13]

II

Let us begin by examining the first of the three contexts I mentioned:

(i) *Intellectual Enquiry:*

Marlowe's and Goethe's Faust are both alienated from their intellectual enquiries. They can find no satisfaction in them. Goethe's Faust asks, "Shall I then rank with gods?" but replies,

> Too well I feel
> My kinship with the worm, who bores the soil,
> Who feeds on dust until the wanderer's heel
> Gives sepulture to all his care and toil.
>   Is it not dust, that fills my hundred shelves,
> And walls me in like any pedant hack?
> Fellow of moth that flits and worm that delves,
> I drag my life through learned bric-a-brak.
> And shall I here discover what I lack
> And learn, by reading countless volumes through,
> That mortals mostly live on misery's rack,
> That happiness is known to just a few?
>
> [Night • Faust's Study (i), pp. 52-53]

Similarly, Marlowe's Faustus can find no satisfaction in logic, physics, law, or theology.

> Is to dispute well logic's chiefest end?

---

13. Goethe, *Faust/Part One*, trans. Philip Wayne (Harmondsworth: Penguin Books, 1976) All references are to this edition.

> Affords this art no greater miracle?
> Then read no more: thou hast attained that end.
>
> [1.1.8-10]

Why is Faust alienated from his studies? The answer lies in
the fact that Faust does not give himself to his studies. On the
contrary, his studies serve to feed his egocentricity. It is sometimes said that intellectual study develops character. This is
unobjectionable, but must be stated carefully. If a student's
character is developed, it is not because the student has spent
much time thinking about the development of his character.
On the contrary, the development of character is shown in the
way a man gives himself to his subject, to the problems in
hand. In doing so a man does not think of his own character
at all. A man gives himself to his subject. Whether he is successful or not, whether his studies bear fruit – that is not within
his control. Put religiously, he would say that that is in God's
hands. What form does patience take here? Patience would be
the conviction that enquiry, engagement with the subject, is
worthwhile despite the ups and downs, despite the outcome.
This is precisely what Faust lacks. He cannot put enquiry first;
he cannot risk the contingency of the outcome. He must
triumph. So although he may put aside many worldly goods,
egocentricity still rules: enquiry must triumph through him.
He cannot abide the long arduous toil connected with enquiry.
He wants a shortcut, instant success. This is the promise of
magic with which the Evil Angel tempts Marlowe's Faustus:

> Go forward, Faustus, in that famous art
> Wherein all nature's treasure is contain'd.
> Be thou on earth as Jove is in the sky,
> Lord and commander of these elements.
>
> [1.1. 74-77]

Faustus is dazzled by the idea of knowing everything:

> How am I glutted with conceit of this!
> Shall I make spirits fetch me what I please,
> Resolve me of all ambiguities,
> Perform what desperate enterprise I will?
>
> [1.1. 78-81]

The conclusion he reaches is inevitable:

> Philosophy is odious and obscure,
> Both law and physic are for petty wits;
> Divinity is basest of the three,
> Unpleasant, harsh, contemptible, and vile.
> 'Tis magic, magic that hath ravish'd me.
>
> [1.1. 106-110]

Yet, ravished or not, magic could not bring intellectual satisfaction. This is because this satisfaction cannot be separated from the course which intellectual enquiries take. One cannot simply have the satisfaction without the intellectual labor. For example, simply being provided with a list of so-called philosophical theses, answers, would be quite meaningless and unrewarding. Unless you appreciated how these theses had emerged from philosophical problems, unless you had felt the philosophical puzzlement which urges one to take this or some other direction, the mere list of so-called answers would be quite meaningless. Instant magic then is no substitute for intellectual enquiry and cannot remove the alienation from enquiry which Faust suffers from. The only remedy for that is for Faust, or anyone else for that matter, to give himself again to the subject in question, to intellectual endeavor.

In this first context of intellectual enquiry we have seen that what patience amounts to cannot be explained in isolation from what commitment to intellectual enquiry involves. Similarly, the lack of patience which may verge on the demonic must be understood against the same background. One of the earliest lessons Marlowe's Faustus has to learn is that hell is not some other realm, the kind of realm which inspires interest in the occult for example, but rather a possible dimension of life as we know it. When Mephistopilis appears to him Faustus asks, "How comes it then that thou art out of hell?" Comes the reply:

> Why, this is hell, nor am I out of it.
> Think'st thou that I who saw the face of God
> And tasted the eternal joys of heaven,
> Am not tormented with ten thousand hells

> In being deprived of everlasting bliss?
> Oh, Faustus, leave these frivolous demands,
> Which strike a terror to my fainting soul.
>
> [1.3. 76-80]

Those who make hell a matter of curiousity about the occult trivialize it. When Goethe's Faust conjures up Mephistopheles, anticipating his coming in many dreadful forms, he finds that when he does appear it is as a fellow scholar:

> So, that is then the essence of the brute!
> A travelling scholar?   Time for laughter yet!
>
> [Faust's Study (ii), p. 74]

The irony is that it is not a time for laughter at all. The demonic appears, unsurprisingly, in the very mode of Faust's own alienation, alienation from intellectual enquiry.

(ii) *Love:*

To see the form which lack of patience takes where love is concerned it is helpful to consider comments made by Kierke-gaard on what is meant by trying to take eternity by storm or trying to foreshorten eternity. Just as in the case of intellec-tual enquiry where its fruits were yielded only to those who gave themselves to the subject in question, so with love. The lover must give himself to the object of his love. Where pos-session is the main aim, come what may, what we have is not love, but seduction. As in the case of intellectual enquiry, so in the case of love, a man may become impatient with the waiting and attention on the other. He wants to achieve his goal immediately; he wants to foreshorten love, take it by storm. It is likely that such a man is in the grip of romanti-cism, thinking that the intensity of love is like the intensity of a pain, or that the firmness of friendship is like the firmness of a handshake. The intensity of the pain or the pressure of the hand is given in the moment, complete, once and for all. Love cannot be completed or given once and for all like that. That is why it is said to labor long and is called kind. Those who think that love can be possessed in an instant can make little sense of the demands of love. Using an example of Kierkegaard's one can say that

> It is here as when an artist sketches a country. The sketch cannot be as big as the country, it must be infinitely smaller; but on that account it also becomes all the easier for the observer to scan the outlines of that country. And yet it may well happen to the observer, if suddenly he were actually set down in that country where the many, many miles really exist and are valid, that he would be unable to recognize the country, or to make any sense of it, or as a traveller, to find his way about in it.[14]

This is not entirely true of Goethe's depiction of Faust. He is in the middle, in a state of tension. Certainly there is evidence of his desire to take love by storm:

> Spare me, Professor Plausible, your saws
> And plaguey discourse on the moral laws.
> To cut the story short, I tell you plain,
> Unless her sweet young loveliness has lain
> Within my arms' embrace this very night,
> The stroke of twelve shall end our pact outright.
>
> [A Street, p. 122]

That is what he wants, "to cut the story short," to foreshorten love, and that is precisely what cannot be done. You cannot cut the story short and still have the same story. Faust and Mephistopheles discuss strategies and techniques together, but they cannot be discussing love. There may be techniques in seduction, but are there techniques in love? But all thought of technique is gone when he gazes at Margareta lying in her bed. He is conscious of the fact that the love she inspires in him ill accords with his designs:

> And you, good Sir: your purpose here, your quest?
> How moved and troubled is my cloudy breast!
> What make you here? Why is your heart so sore?
> Ah, wretched Faust, I know you now no more!

---

14. *Purity of Heart*, p. 114.

> And what enchanted atmosphere is this?
> I thought to follow hot on passion's flair,
> And now I languish for a true-love's bliss:
>
> [Evening, p. 125]

When Mephistopheles tries to reduce all this to lewdity Faust
cries, "Shame on you, man!" He is far removed from Mephistopheles's sinister response:

> Ah, now you're put about,
> And claim the moral right to cry 'For shame',
> Because chaste ears must never hear the name
> Of things chaste hearts will never go without.
> But patience, friend, and let us still be lenient:
> Lie to yourself whenever it's convenient.
>
> [Forest and Cavern, p. 147]

That is too hard on Faust. Nevertheless, we cannot, as we have
seen, go to the other extreme, and say that he has given himself to the object of his love. The self is still central in his concern and this means that he is alienated from love. Recognizing
this himself he realizes that he cannot bring to Margareta what
normal love could — that love which Margareta has:

> What means that ecstasy upon her breast?
> What though her bosom lulls my heart to rest —
> Do I not know myself to be her doom?
> I, the uprooted, I the homeless jade,
> The monster I, whose only aim is this:
> To scour the rocks like any blind cascade
> Racing and eager for the dark abyss.
> While she from passion sweetly lived aloof,
> With senses of a scarcely wakened child,
> The alpine paddock and the cottage roof
> Her busy tender world and undefiled.
> And I, the curse of God upon my brow.
> I, not content
> To grip the rocks and make them bow
> And leave them rent,
> Must undermine her innocence as well,
> And make of her a sacrifice for Hell.
> Help, Devil, to cut short the agony.

Whatever is to come, let quickly come.
Now may her fate come crashing down on me,
And drag her with me to the self-same doom!

[Forest and Cavern, pp. 149-150]

(iii) *Morality:*

In discussing the distinction between patience and impatience
in intellectual enquiry and love I have stressed how attempts to
come to knowledge directly in either sphere by shortcutting
the arduous routes by which such knowledge is arrived at are
bound to end in confusion and frustration. Kierkegaard discussed a man who will do anything to attain honor. He cannot
attain it in this way, of course, since honor is incompatible with
doing anything whatsoever. So although a man may seem to
possess honor by reputation, what he has is always appearance
rather than reality. The same point could be made by saying
that what he has is an external relation to honor rather than an
internal relation. This distinction can be usefully applied to a
discussion of Faust's relation to moral considerations. For much
of the time that relation is an external one.

Marlow's Faustus is skeptical as to whether God can harm
him, but he understands this externally:

When Mephostophilis shall stand by me,
What God can hurt me? Faustus, thou art safe.

[2.1. 25-26]

It is almost as if God and the Devil are both to strike a blow,
leaving the victim to assess which blow hurts him the more.
Here, there would be a common conception of harm which
would assess God and the Devil. Sometimes the way Marlowe
writes aids this confused comparison:

GOOD ANGEL. Never too late, if Faustus will repent.
EVIL ANGEL. If thou repent devils will tear thee in pieces.
GOOD ANGEL. Repent, and they shall never raze thy skin.

[2.2. 82-84]

Given such argument it does look as if the soul goes to the
highest bidder. The language does not allow the point to be
made that the harm the Devil can make is the degradation of

the soul, whereas God's wrath is separation from grace. In other words, there is no one common conception of harm which transcends the two cases. Faustus, on the other hand, thinks only of harm in terms of the satisfaction of his wordly desires. When he begins to worry he puts his doubts aside with the thought,

> Tush, Christ did call the thief upon the cross;
> Then rest thee, Faustus, quiet in conceit.
>
> [4.4.26-27]

He speaks here as if repentance could be made a matter of policy, a matter of decision, now that time is running out. But, then, of course, it would not be repentance. Kierkegaard says that those who speak of repenting at the eleventh hour as a matter of prudent policy reduce an important truth to a crudity:

> When remorse awakens concern, whether it be in the youth or the old man, it awakens it always at the eleventh hour. It is not deceived by a false notion of a long life, for it is the eleventh hour. And in the eleventh hour one understands life in a wholly different way than in the days of youth or in the busy time of manhood or in the final moment of old age. He who repents at any other hour of the day repents in the temporal sense.[15]

In other words, he has only the show or appearance of repentance, not the reality. When a man really repents, the very fact that he needed to do so means that it was getting late for him as a person — it was the eleventh hour. Even at the end Faustus's understanding remains within the temporal:

> Ah Faustus,
> Now hast thou but one bare hour to live,
> And then thou must be damn'd perpetually.
> Stand still, you ever-moving spheres of heaven,
> That time may cease and midnight never come.
> Fair nature's eye, rise, rise again, and make
> Perpetual day. Or let this hour be but
> A year, a month, a week, a natural day,

---

15. Ibid., p. 41.

That Faustus may repent and save his soul.
O lente, lente, currite noctis equi!
The stars move still, time runs, the clock will strike.
The devil will come, and Faustus must be damn'd.

[5.2. 134-145]

The only hope here is that time will stand still. There is no understanding here of Kierkegaard's remark that when a man repents the clock always shows the same time — eleven o'clock. The irony of *O lente, lente . . .* is that it is taken from Ovid's *Amores* "where the lover wishes that night should never end so that he may lie with his mistress for ever."[16] So ends Marlowe's Faustus.

Goethe's Faust is a more complex character. We have already noted some of the tensions he undergoes in his relationship with Margareta. Similar tensions can be found in the pull between self-renunciation and self-fulfillment in his soul:

The pain of life, that haunts our narrow way,
I cannot shed with this or that attire.
Too old am I to be content with play,
Too young to live untroubled by desire.
What comfort can the shallow world bestow?
Renunciation! — Learn, man, to forgo!
This is the lasting theme of themes,
That soon or late will show its power,
The tune that lurks in all our dreams,
And the hoarse whisper of each hour.
Yet, each new day I shudder when I wake
With bitter tears to look upon the sun,
Knowing that in the journey he will make
None of my longings will come true, not one.

[Faust's Study, pp. 82-83]

But, despite the tensions, in the end in the Prison Scene with Margareta it is clear that external considerations are the ones that prevail. Margareta sees the freedom of the soul in moral

---

16. See Marlowe, *The Complete Plays* (Harmondsworth: Penguin Books, 1976), p. 336n.

terms. Can she be free given what she has done? For Faust, freedom is simply physical freedom from prison.

> MARGARETA. You freed me from my chain,
> Indeed you took me to your heart again;
> How comes it that you have no dread of me?
> Or know you not the creature that you free?
> FAUST. Nay, come!
> Dawn softens night, the deepest shades are fled.
> MARGARETA. My mother, by my hand, lies dead;
> Dead is my child, that I did drown. . . .
> FAUST. Let the past be! The terrors it will start!
> Dear, you will break my heart.
>
> [Prison, p. 193]

Margareta understands her condition and her needs in terms of her guilt and need for repentance. These matters remain external considerations for Faust. In the end, although she refuses to escape she is redeemed on high. We are back to the beginning of our discussion of patience and Kierkegaard's question of how a person can will the unavoidable; how a person who is captive can nevertheless be free. Faust who is physically free is, in the moral sense, captive. Margareta has patience by which, as Kierkegaard says, "the prisoner effects his freedom — although not in the sense that need make the jailer anxious or fearful."[17] Faust eludes the jailer's grasp and yet is captive. Surely, here at the end of the first part of Goethe's *Faust* is an instance of what is meant by saying that he who seeks to save his life loses it, but he who seeks to lose his life for God's sake, saves it. Margareta says, "Into God's hand my trembling soul I give."

In the three contexts I have discussed, intellectual enquiry, love, and morality, I have tried to give some indication of what the distinction between patience and lack of patience comes to. The alienation from the good which this lack of patience involves cannot be righted by external means. One cannot get nearer intellectual enquiry, love, or morality by heaping up more and more external inducements. One is no nearer than

---

17. *Purity of Heart*, p. 173.

when the first inducement was made. One is in a state of what Kierkegaard calls infinite approximation. Sometimes Goethe's Faust recognizes this:

> In vain I gathered human treasure,
> And all that mortal spirit could digest:
> I come at last to recognize my measure,
> And know the sterile desert in my breast.
> I have not raised myself one poor degree,
> Nor stand I nearer to infinity.
>
> [Faust's Study (iii), p. 91]

The trouble is precisely the sterile desert in the breast. This can only be changed by a radical change of perspective — by what is external becoming internal. Marlowe's Faust must give up seeing hell in external terms:

> Nay, and this be hell, I'll willingly be damn'd.
> What! Sleeping, eating, walking and disputing?
>
> [2.1. 141-142]

Yet it is precisely in the way in which they impinge on sleeping, eating, walking, disputing, and loving, in short, on human life, that the categories of the spiritual and the demonic have their meaning. Patience is one form the spiritual may take and I have shown how this would involve, in the contexts we have discussed, a giving of oneself to intellectual enquiry, love, and moral considerations. This being so, the nature of Goethe's Faust's pact with the Devil may puzzle us, since he promises to be the Devil's,

> If to the fleeting hour I say
> 'Remain, so fair thou art, remain!'
> Then bind me with your fatal chain,
> For I will perish in that day.
>
> [Faust's Study (iii), p. 87]

Yet, there is no contradiction, since the giving of oneself referred to here is that of premature indulgent resignation rather than the kind we have been discussing.[18]

---

18. I owe this observation to my colleague D. L. Sims, Philip Wayne offers this interpretation too in his Introduction to Goethe, *Faust/Part One*, p. 17.

Finally, one matter must be made absolutely clear. Nothing I have said about patience and impatience should be taken to mean that this distinction is easy to draw in one's own life, or in other people's lives. Whether renunciation is called for and whether one should forgo, or whether one should wipe away the bitter tears with which one looks upon the sun and do something about all the longings which have not come true, not one — that is possibly one of the hardest decisions a person may be called upon to make.

8/MEANING, MEMORY, AND LONGING

PHILOSOPHERS AND LITERARY CRITICS ALIKE are interested in the ways in which people may lose their hold on certain ways of thinking, perspectives, or modes of thought. Concern with such loss is central in the works of writers who are said to make up The Theatre of the Absurd. But what does the loss amount to, and what kind of concern can it occasion? These are some of the questions which Martin Esslin tackles in his book *The Theatre of the Absurd*.[1] Unfortunately, Esslin's allegiance to a priori theses obscures the very phenomena about which he wants to enlighten us.

Esslin puts forward a thesis according to which language is inherently inadequate, and human life, dominated by that language, inevitably meaningless. In this essay this thesis is criticized. It will be argued that if we want to refer to lost, distorted, or perverted meanings, there must be *some* reference to the meaningful in human life. This is not to deny, as we shall see, that the reference may have to be via memory or longing.

Esslin is quite right when he says on the first page of his Preface that "the type of theatre discussed in this book is by no means of concern only to a narrow circle of intellectuals" (p. 13). His reason for saying this, however, is because he believes that this type of theatre "may provide a new language, new ideas, new approaches, and a new vitalized philosophy to transform the modes of thought and feeling of the public at large in a not too distant future" (p. 13). Not only does Esslin

---

1. Martin Esslin, *The Theatre of the Absurd* (Harmondsworth: Penguin Books, 1977). All references are from this edition.

suggest that new values, new ideas, new philosophies should come out of this type of theatre; he also suggests that the standards by which these should be understood and judged are also to be determined by the character of the theatre involved: "They can be judged only by the standards of the Theatre of the Absurd, which it is the purpose of this book to define and clarify" (p. 22). Yet, these standards are not the standards of a group or of a school. "On the contrary," Esslin tells us, "each of the writers in question is an individual who regards himself as a lone outsider, cut off and isolated in his private world" (p. 22).

If these claims about the isolation of the artist were taken strictly, the theatrical works could not speak to us or have any significance for us. But we need not take Esslin's claims for the private, self-authenticating validity of these theatrical works very seriously, since he himself goes on to say of the dramatists that "if they also, very clearly and in spite of themselves, have a good deal in common, it is because their work sensitively mirrors and reflects the preoccupations and anxieties, the emotions and thinking of their contemporaries in the Western world" (p. 22). So after all we are talking about a public, recognizable cultural phenomenon.

One of the main characteristics of the phenomenon Esslin wants to explore is anxiety. What does this anxiety amount to? It is supposed to be anxiety concerning lost perspectives on life and a consequent bewilderment about what could be meaningful. Esslin's initial characterization of this situation fails to capture its character. His tone is that of a brisk positivist, newly shed of metaphysical illusions: "The hallmark of this attitude is its sense that the certitudes and unshakable basic assumptions of former ages have been swept away, that they have been tested and found wanting, that they have been discredited as cheap and somewhat childish illusions" (p. 23). The emphasis here is on something found rather than on something lost, on liberation rather than bewilderment. If the old meanings are discredited, if they were cheap and childish, how can there be any sense of loss which is not itself cheap or childish?

Surely, on this view, enlightenment has rescued men from the darkness of superstition.

When we examine the writings by which Esslin hopes to illustrate his thesis, we see that they are far more complex than his gloss on them would suggest. He quotes from Camus, Ionesco, and Beckett to support his case. First, Camus in *The Myth of Sisyphys:* "A world that can be explained by reasoning, however faulty, is a familiar world. But, in a universe that is suddenly deprived of illusions and of light, man feels a stranger. He is an irremediable exile, because he is deprived of memories of a lost homeland as much as he lacks the hope of a promised land to come. This divorce between man and his life, the actor and his setting, truly constitutes the feeling of Absurdity."[2] Ionesco defines 'absurd' as "that which is devoid of purpose. . . . Cut off from his religious, metaphysical, and transcendental roots, man is lost; all his actions become senseless, absurd, useless."[3] Beckett in his study of Proust says that "if love . . . is a function of man's sadness, friendship is a function of his cowardice; and if neither can be realized because of the impenetrability (isolation) of all that is not '*cosa mentale*', at least the failure to possess may have the nobility of that which is tragic, whereas the attempt to communicate where no communication is possible is merely a simian vulgarity, or horribly comic, like the madness that holds a conversation with the furniture."[4] In this context, for Proust, "the artistic tendency is not expansive, but a contraction. And art is the apotheosis of solitude. There is no communication because there are no vehicles of communication."[5]

There is little trace of Esslin's brisk positivism in these remarks. Camus speaks of lost illusions, but also of lost light. He does not say that the lights that shone in the past are neces-

---

2. Albert Camus, *Le Mythe de Sisyphe*, p. 18, Esslin's translation, at p. 23. Cf. Camus, *The Myth of Sisyphys and Other Essays*, p. 5.

3. Eugene Ionesco, "Dans les armes de la ville," *Cahiers de la Compagnie Madeleine Renaud–Jean-Louis Barrault*, Paris, No. 20, October 1957; at p. 23.

4. Samuel Beckett, *Proust*, p. 46; at p. 32.

5. Ibid., p. 47; at pp 32–33.

sarily illusory. What he says is that they do not or cannot shine now. Ionesco simply says that man is lost and rootless now. Why this is so has yet to be explored. Proust is not giving us the essence of love or friendship, but telling us, in very specific ways, what love or friendship may become. Esslin himself says that " 'Absurd' originally means 'out of harmony' in a musical context" (p. 23), and emphasizes that the use of the term in the plays he is considering has nothing in common with its use when signifying what is ridiculous. But if we want to talk of things being 'out of harmony', there must be some story to tell in terms of lost, distorted, or perverted meanings. No dogmatic thesis which claims that meaninglessness is the necessary lot of human beings can do justice to the complexity of such stories.

Esslin gets close to such a thesis when he develops his argument by saying that there are further distinctions which must be made between Camus and Sartre on the one hand, and the Theatre of the Absurd on the other:

> If Camus argued that in our disillusioned age the world has ceased to make sense, he did so in the elegantly rationalistic and discursive style of an eighteenth-century moralist, in well-constructed and polished plays. If Sartre argues that existence comes before essence and that human personality can be reduced to pure potentiality and the freedom to choose itself anew at any moment, he presents his ideas in plays based on brilliantly drawn characters who remain wholly consistent and thus reflect the old convention that each human being has a core of immutable, unchanging essence — in fact, an immortal soul. And the beautiful phrasing and argumentative brilliance of both Sartre and Camus in their relentless probing still, by implication, proclaim a tacit convention that logical discourse can offer valid solutions, that the analysis of language will lead to the uncovering of basic concepts — Platonic ideas. (pp. 24-25)

The Theatre of the Absurd by contrast, it is claimed, "strives to express its sense of the senselessness of the human condition and the inadequacy of the rational approach by the open abandonment of rational devices and discursive thought" (p. 24).

These remarks need sifting. It will surprise readers of Camus and Sartre to find them described as wanting to unearth Platonic ideas. Camus and Sartre reacted against slavish conventionalism and mindless habit. Both were tempted to think that this could be done by placing the individual outside all conventions and habits, and by endowing him with one free unadulterated act — the power to choose. We are reminded of the only sure freedom remaining for the individual after Descartes's methodological doubt has run its course — the freedom to doubt. Yet, a little reflection shows how problematic these concepts are. Who is this individual placed beyond everything that makes life recognizably human? He is supposed to belong to nothing. In that case, what is his choice to consist in? If we were simply told to choose, we should be at a loss in the absence of definite circumstances to make obvious the import of the invitation. It is no accident that a baby could not enter the realms of discourse for the first time with the words, "I choose it," any more than he could with the words, "I doubt it." Until the child has been told something, until he understands something, there is nothing to occasion the child's doubt or choice. Both doubt and choice are occasioned and therefore cannot be the fundamental concepts in terms of which human life is to be understood. Unless we already cared for something, there would be no occasions for choice. It could be argued that whereas Sartre never resolves these problems, Camus does so only by giving up his initial metaphysical assumptions. Since many of his early characters operate according to sheer choice, he can portray little more than caprice. To give life to some of the moral and political concerns of his later works, he has to give up the individualistic aestheticism which basked in the warmth of the Algerian sun, and take account of those ideas which, for better or for worse, have entered into the lives of men.[6]

Although there are undoubted differences between Camus and Sartre, and the writers Esslin wants to discuss, are they helpfully marked by saying that the latter have in common "the open abandonment of rational devices and discursive

6. I was helped to appreciate this point by a hitherto unpublished essay on Camus' novels by Anthony Duff and Sandra Marshall.

thought"? These writers may well want to depict those who are even less at home in their world than those who Camus and Sartre show to us. The language which they use may well break with many conventions. Yet, no break can be so radical that *no* connections remain. If no connections remain, how can we have any sense of lost, distorted, perverted, or barely glimpsed meanings? It must not be thought that this observation secures a place for the meaningful in human life by means of a logical contrast. There could be a world in which, while utilitarian concerns make sense, much else is dark confusion. No philosophy can rule out the possibility of the human race going mad. Certainly, there would be no statement of it in a literature! Similarly, if modes of thought which were once meaningful are *completely* lost, there could not be an expression of this loss in literature. How could there be? If the sense of loss persists, it must be conveyed through memory, bewilderment, or some such phenomenon. Still, it is also possible to convey a meaninglessness more radical than that derived from a sense of loss. On an individualistic level, a man may be said to be born out of his time; he does not feel at home in his world. He cannot say what he is looking for. All he knows is that he is not at home in any of *this*. To be depicted in literature, such a person still has to refer to the various ways in which people live their lives. His perspective, however, will be that of a stranger. *Ex hypothesi,* such a character cannot be depicted as the free, liberated man. On the contrary, he looks for a city, but has no idea what its foundations might be. The most he can say is that he has not found it. For this to be conveyed in literature there must be some expression of the relation between the person's uprootedness and the ways of living from which he feels cut off. The writers Esslin discusses want to show what happens when the estrangement is not individualistic, but becomes pervasive in a culture. People will not feel at home in their world, will not feel that the moves they go through really matter, and yet, they will be unable to say in what direction the remedy lies. Here, the meaningful is present by virtue of its absence. In this context, the contrast between the meaningful and the meaningless is not shown in terms of the meaningless present and the memory of lost meanings, but in terms of an inarticulate longing for something different from what is possessed at present. In either case, it is woefully inadequate to mark the difference between the Theatre of the Absurd and the plays which preceded it by saying that "if a good play relies on witty repartee and pointed dialogue, these often consist of incoherent babblings" (p. 22).

II

The general points made hitherto can be emphasized by turning to Esslin's discussion of Beckett. Here, too, we have contradictory tendencies. On the one hand, Esslin is aware that Beckett is showing how certain hopes and expectations cannot be expressed in our time. This is an observation on a present state. On the other hand, time and again, Esslin turns these particularities into a general thesis about the inherent meaninglessness of this or that. This is to miss the force of what Beckett is doing. For example, if Beckett is showing what certain forms of language have become, this is simply obscured by a general thesis about the inherent meaninglessness of language. Beckett is often exposing an unwarranted ease in the language, but this is shown in terms of the language he uses. To illustrate this thesis, let us examine it in three contexts in *Waiting for Godot:* the notion of waiting, human relationships, and language.

(a) *The Notion of Waiting*

In *Waiting for Godot,* as Esslin says, a static situation is explored: "On a country road, by a tree, two old tramps, Vladimir and Estragon, are waiting. That is the opening situation at the beginning of act I. At the end of act I they are informed that Mr. Godot, with whom they believe they have an appointment, cannot come, but that he will surely come tomorrow (p. 45). Later, Esslin says of this situation, which does not change throughout the play:

The subject of the play is not Godot but waiting, the act of waiting as an essential and characteristic aspect of the human condition. Throughout our lives we always wait for something, and Godot simply represents the objective of our waiting — an event, a thing, a person, death. Moreover, it is in the act of waiting that we experience the flow of *time* in its purest, most evident form. If we are active, we tend to forget the passage of time, we *pass* the time, but if we are merely passively waiting, we are confronted with the action of time itself. (p. 49)

There are many kinds of "waiting." A religious promise is given to those "who wait on the Lord," where the waiting amounts to a kind of patience.[7] The individual who waits in this way is told: "He will give thee thy heart's desire." Simone Weil explores this kind of waiting in *Waiting on God*. There is nothing passive about it. She contrasts it with a very different kind of waiting which she believes many people feed on, namely, waiting for something to turn up which will compensate for some ill which has come their way. They wait for a rectification of the balance. Sometimes, these expectations can appear in reverse form. I once knew a college porter who invariably said on sunny days, "We'll have to pay for this later." Usually, however, the waiting is for some kind of compensation, whether or not this takes a religious form.[8] This waiting too is not particularly passive. The horror of death, for Nikolay Stepanovitch, in Chekhov's *A Dreary Story*, comes from the realization that there is to be no compensation. Waiting which is religious or secular need not take this form. A secular counterpart to Simone Weil's discussion of waiting on God can be found in Sorel's *Reflections on Violence*. In Sorel the revolutionary aim is not realizable, but it characterizes the direction and the spirit in which the revolutionary travels.

The waiting in which Esslin is interested is a passive waiting in which we experience "the flow of *time* in its purest, most evident form." Despite the fact that realization is not central to

7. I explore this notion of patience in "Knowledge, Patience, and Faust" in this collection.

8. See the treatment of the desire for compensation in "Philosophizing and Reading a Story" in this collection.

what Sorel means by "the spirit of the journey," the constant striving he advocates is unintelligible apart from the ideals which inform it. What we need is something more passive. This is achieved when we sever the connection between waiting and its object; when the people involved have no clear conception of what they are waiting for. This is precisely the situation with Vladimir and Estragon.

Now according to Esslin's argument this passive waiting should give us the purest experience of time. He contrasts this with the evasion of this experience which absorption in activities involves: "If we are active, we tend to forget the passage of time, we *pass* the time." This comment recalls pastimes — cardplaying during a long train journey, for example — which people may indulge in to make the time pass quickly. But why should all activities be regarded in this way? To insist that they must be so regarded is simply the kind of dogmatism against which we should protest. When people give themselves to various activities, not passively or mindlessly, but because they are absorbed in their characteristic interests and problems, they can be described with good reason as "making the most of their time." We cannot deny the phenomenon which Esslin rightly describes as "passing the time," but why does he ignore the phenomenon describable as "making the most of one's time"? By doing so he can speak of "an essential and characteristic aspect of the human condition," although at other times he wants to deny that there is such a thing as the essence of human nature.

If waiting did not sometimes have a point, we could not have a successful portrayal of pointless waiting. For Vladimir and Estragon the waiting *is* in vain, precisely because they have no clear conception of anything that could inform it. Esslin quotes a passage which should have enabled him to see this: "Nothing happens, nobody comes, nobody goes, it's awful" (p. 45). So far from such a state revealing the flow of time in its purest form, it reveals the terror of a time without meaning. What Beckett shows cannot be *presented* as a comprehensive category. Such a depiction of "pure waiting" is as problematic as Descartes's "pure doubting" or Sartre's "pure choosing." Yet, it is such a depiction that Esslin attempts. The objectless waiting that Beckett depicts, on the other hand, gets its force by contrast with an absent meaning, an absence portrayed by memory of the past or inarticulate longing for the future. Constructing general theses as Esslin does obscures the particularity of what Beckett wants to show us.

(b) *Human Relationships*

Esslin argues that Beckett raises the issue of personal identity. He does so by showing how his characters have difficulty in recognizing one another. Esslin describes the phenomenon well:

> If Godot is the object of Vladimir's and Estragon's desire, he seems naturally ever beyond their reach. It is significant that the boy who acts as go-between fails to recognize the pair from day to day. The French version explicitly states that the boy who appears in the second act is the same boy as the one in the first act, yet the boy denies that he has ever seen the two tramps before and insists that this is the first time he has acted as Godot's messenger. As the boy leaves, Vladimir tries to impress it upon him: "You're sure you saw me, eh, you won't come and tell me tomorrow that you never saw me before?" The boy does not reply, and we know that he will again fail to recognize them. Can we ever be sure that the human beings we meet are the same today as they were yesterday? When Pozzo and Lucky first appear, neither Vladimir nor Estragon seems to recognize them; Estragon even takes Pozzo for Godot. But after they have gone, Vladimir comments that they have changed since their last appearance. Estragon insists that he didn't know them.
>
> VLADIMIR: Yes you do know them.
> ESTRAGON: No I don't know them.
> VLADIMIR: We know them, I tell you. You forget everything.
>   (*Pause. To himself*) Unless they're not the same . . .
> ESTRAGON: Why didn't they recognize us, then?
> VLADIMIR: That means nothing. I too pretended not to recognize them. And then nobody ever recognizes us.
>
> In the second act, when Pozzo and Lucky reappear, cruelly deformed by the action of time, Vladimir and Estragon again have their doubts whether they are the same people they met

on the previous day. Nor does Pozzo remember them: "I don't remember having met anyone yesterday. But tomorrow I won't remember having met anybody today." (pp. 50-51)

These are undoubtedly important matters. They can be illustrated by a discussion of parallel cases. Is the question of whether a person has a claim on another from one day to the next one which can be resolved purely in theoretical terms? The following quotation from a discussion of authority and revelation in Kierkegaard brings out why this question has to be given a negative answer:

But if we briefly consider a concept which has fascinated contemporary philosophy — namely, the concept of promise — we might better understand what Kierkegaard meant by an 'ethical investigation'. When a person says 'I promise', then in most cases, or as a rule, we do consider him bound, morally bound, by his promise. The utterance of these words, as a rule, brings the speaker under an obligation. Of course, people do also speak loosely and insincerely and will sometimes use these words even when they have no intention of trying to fulfill the promise. But in such cases we nevertheless hold them responsible for what they say; responsible for the deception involved in saying 'I promise' without any intention of actually promising and being bound by the promise. Now in making comments of this sort about the use of 'promise' I think we are noting ethical considerations embedded in the concept of promise; this would be an aspect of what Kierkegaard might call an ethical investigation of the concept of promise.

But now suppose that over a period of time many people came to use 'I promise' as though they meant 'I will if it is convenient'. They no longer felt morally bound to keep promises beyond what convenience might allow. Would we not have in this case something like 'having forgotten' what it is to promise, or having forgotten the concept of promise? While people still said 'I promise' on innumerable occasions, they had forgotten how to promise without regard to convenience. Confronted with a situation such as this, I think we can appreciate the difficulty of undertaking to recover the concept of promise, of trying to reeducate people with regard to the practice of promising without regard to convenience. Likewise we should be able to appreciate Kierkegaard's concern for the forgetfulness and confusion which become evident when folk speak of themselves as Christians and use the terms of Christian discourse, yet now in diminished senses and without awareness of the incongruity between their speaking and living and the Christian faith.

But Kierkegaard's situation was even more complex than this. Not only was there a forgetfulness present in the careless and loose use of Christian terms, but there were also philosophers and theologians about who were offering new interpretations of Christian terms. The analogy to this would be philosophers coming on the scene to declare that the real and abiding essence of the concept of promise is the intention to do if convenient.[9]

If the redefinitions became pervasive we should have to say that this is what a promise has become. Instead of asking, in a theoretical way, what is the essence of promise-keeping, all we can do is to ask what it is to keep a promise. There may be practices or traditions which enable us to comment on the character of promise-keeping within them, but no answer in the abstract about the essence of promise-keeping would be helpful. So the mere uttering of the words, "Remember me? You promised me ... " would have no magic hold in themselves. They cannot be made effective as if by what Wittgenstein called "a baptism of meaning." Everything depends on how these words bear on other features of people's lives — on how they bear on convenience, for example.

It does not take much to see how these points also apply to the question of human identity and relationships. Who a person is and what relationships he has with others — these too cannot be determined by a baptism of meaning. There is an amusing illustration of this in *Waiting for Godot*. Pozzo wants to show that he is someone of importance, but it is as if he thinks this can be made secure by the mere uttering of his name. Beckett shows the futility of this idle hope in the reactions of Vladimir and Estragon.

POZZO: (*terrifying voice*). I am Pozzo! (*Silence.*) Pozzo! (*Si-*

9. Joe R. Jones, "Some Remarks on Authority and Revelation in Kierkegaard," *The Journal of Religion* 57, no. 3 (July 1977), 234–235.

lence.) Does that name mean nothing to you? (*Silence.*)
I say does that name mean nothing to you?
Vladimir and Estragon look at each other questioningly.
ESTRAGON: (*pretending to search*) Bozzo . . . Bozzo . . .
VLADIMIR: (*ditto*). Pozzo . . . Pozzo . . .
POZZO: PPPOZZZO!
ESTRAGON: Ah! Pozzo . . . let me see . . . Pozzo . . .
VLADIMIR: It is Pozzo or Bozzo?
ESTRAGON: Pozzo . . . no . . . I'm afraid I . . . no . . . I don't seem
to . . .
Pozzo advances threatingly.
VLADIMIR: (*conciliating*). I once knew a family called Gozzo.
The mother had the clap.[10]

At other points in the play, while Vladimir or Estragon are
sure of pain in their own case individually, they have doubts
whether the other is in pain. What is it to believe that another
is in pain divorced of all reactions to pain? What is it to commit
oneself to someone divorced of all future implications? How
could promises made in sexual encounters mean anything if the
people involved may not even greet each other the following
day? It would mean little to say, "Remember what you said last
night?" The reply would simply be, "But that was yesterday."
One person would not recognize another as far as any claims
are concerned from one day to the next. As Pozzo says, "I
don't remember having met anyone yesterday. But tomorrow I
won't remember having met anybody today."[11] Such an isolat-
ing of relationships from a yesterday and a tomorrow attempts
to reduce human emotions to the status of sensations. I can ask,
"How's your headache?" and be told "It's gone today, thank
goodness." But what if I ask, "Did you mean what you said
about love last night?" and receive the same reply — "It's gone
today, thank goodness"? We might say that, as in the case of
the man who used the word 'promise' in a degenerate sense,
this man too stands condemned. But, again, what if this is what
talk of love becomes — talk of a transient sensation? Could we
not say that at least one concept of love has been forgotten?

10. Samuel Beckett, *Waiting for Godot*, pp. 22–23.
11. Ibid., p. 88.

Tendencies in this direction are found in Erica Jong's fantasy of "pure" sexual encounters in *Fear of Flying*. In Robert Alley's *Last Tango in Paris* the trouble comes from the male lover wanting the physical relationship to have a significance which extends into other aspects of life.[12] The woman cannot stand this prospect and kills him when he pursues her, denying that she knows him. Although the denial is false in the sense that she knows that this is the man she has been meeting regularly to enjoy sexual intercourse, her denial has another dimension. She refuses to know him outside the narrow context of the sexual encounter. She refuses to say, "This is the same man as I knew there" and face the consequences. Similarly, in *Waiting for Godot*, the characters, in this same sense, wonder whether they know each other. For example, does a deforming change affect the claims that a person has on one? Consider the many different circumstances and considerations which might lead one person to say, "He has no claim on me anymore. He is not the same person," and another to urge, "Of course he is the same person. You cannot desert him now." Is it clear that this dispute could be settled theoretically? Moral considerations will enter into the determination of what does and does not constitute "the same" and hence into what constitutes a justifiable claim on another. The characters in *Waiting for Godot* do not know any more what considerations should have weight in these matters. When Vladimir and Estragon do express sympathy with Lucky it is of such a capricious and rootless kind that it can be transformed at a stroke to Pozzo, Lucky's tormentor. Given this, can we speak of an expression of sympathy here at all?

Despite the fact that Esslin is sometimes aware of the problems Beckett's characters face, he obscures them by prefacing his description of them with a conception which is purely theoretical in character:

The flow of time confronts us with the basic problem of being
— the problem of the nature of the self, which, being subject
to constant change in time, is in constant flux and therefore

---

12. Tendencies in which emotions are reduced to sensations are explored further in "Ingmar Bergman's Reductionism" in this collection.

ever outside our grasp. . . . Being subject to this process of time flowing through us and changing us in doing so, we are, at no single moment in our lives, identical with ourselves. (pp. 49-50)

This thesis is essentially ahistorical. Since it is one which is supposed to apply to us at any time, it obscures the substantive shifts between a time when people do know who they are and what their obligations to others consist in, and a time when all this has become increasingly problematic. According to Esslin, the matter is necessarily problematic because of the flow of time, so that those who were sure of themselves must have been wrong. Beckett, on the other hand, is concerned with a particular time, our time, and with what he thinks has happened in it. Unless you distinguish between times, such predicaments could not be recorded. Esslin's undifferentiating reference to "the flow of time" would have the same effect.

(c) *Language*

Esslin thinks that Beckett is putting forward a thesis about the inherent inadequacy of language. It is not surprising, therefore, to be told that, on Beckett's view, "nothingness is the only reality" (p. 74). Esslin contrasts *Waiting for Godot* and *Endgame* as follows: "If *Waiting for Godot* shows its two heroes whiling away the time in a succession of desultory, and never-ending, games, Beckett's second play deals with an 'end-game', the final game in the hour of death" (p. 61). This is a serious distortion of what Beckett is showing us, and he rejected it. When English friends first translated the title of his play as "End of the Game," " 'No,' Beckett replied emphatically, 'It is *Endgame*, as in chess'."[13] He was not talking about the end of the game, but about a state of the game. Failing to realize this, Esslin regards his work as a *tour de force* in face of the inherent inadequacy of language. But language has no *inherent* inadequacy. What Beckett shows again and again is how certain forms of language may have a terrible hold on people's lives and the implications for other forms of language when

---

13. See Deirdre Bair, *Samuel Beckett*, p. 467.

this happens. Esslin misses entirely the force of Beckett's reply to Gessner who "asked him about the contradiction between his writing and his obvious conviction that language could not convey meaning": "*Que voulez-vous, Monsieur? C'est les mots; on n'a rien d'autre*" (p. 84). On Esslin's view, "language in Beckett's plays serves to express the breakdown, the disintegration of language. Where there is no certainty, there can be no definite meanings — and the impossibility of ever attaining certainty is one of the main themes of Beckett's plays" (p. 85).

Having drawn these conclusions, however, Esslin admits that other things he wants to say seem paradoxical as a result. He is simply prepared to embrace the paradox:

> But, if Beckett's use of language is designed to devalue language as a vehicle for conceptual thought or as an instrument for the communication of ready-made answers to the problems of the human condition, his continued use of language, must, paradoxically, be regarded as an attempt to communicate on his own part, to communicate the incommunicable.... Beckett's entire work can be seen as a search for a reality that lies behind mere reasoning in conceptual terms. He may have devaluated language as an instrument for the communication of ultimate truths, but he has shown himself a great master of language as an artistic medium. (p. 87)

Esslin does not take seriously enough Ionesco's own reply to a similar charge of contradictoriness. People had said that Ionesco too held that language was incapable of achieving communication, to which he replied, "The very fact of writing and presenting plays is surely incompatible with such a view. I simply held that it is difficult to make oneself understood, not absolutely impossible."[14] Ionesco is recognizing that without some distinction between the meaningful and the meaningless, the difficulties he is referring to could not be portrayed. Esslin himself seems to recognize the need for such distinctions at times, as when he recognizes that revolt needs some kind of background to give it sense: he says that in Genet's *The Maids* "the revolt of the maids against their masters is not a social

---

14. Ionesco, "The Playwright's Role," *Observer*, June 29, 1958.

gesture, a revolutionary action; it is tinged with nostalgia and longing, like the revolt of the fallen angel Satan against the world of light from which he is forever banished" (p. 204).

Esslin's confusion is, at bottom, a simple one. He latches on to an aspect of human discourse which has become problematic for many people, religious discourse, for example, and then elevates this phenomenon into a general thesis about the inherent inadequacy of human discourse as such. In this, we must conclude, with Cavell, that Esslin takes "Beckett's work much as any corrupted audience takes it."[15] Beckett is not trying to communicate the incommunicable, but to communicate a particular state of affairs which is problematic, even absurd. A dramatist can only mark this absurdity, however, if there are connections with deeper things, however elusive the connections may be. This is why Cavell can show us convincingly in his essay on *Endgame* that Beckett

> is not marketing subjectivity, popularizing *angst*, amusing and thereby excusing us with pictures of our psychopathology; he is outlining the facts — of mind, of community — which show why these have become our pastimes. The discovery of *Endgame*, both in topic and technique, is not the failure of meaning (if that means the lack of meaning) but its total, even totalitarian, success — our inability *not* to mean what we are given to mean.[16]

And what we are given to mean is the mediocrities of life — the bitchings and the squabblings, the pettiness and weakness. And it is to the particularity of this deadening detail that Beckett draws our attention. It is a scene, however, which gets its force by virtue of what it makes impossible, by virtue of what it necessarily makes absent.

Esslin's view of language has a telling influence on his summing-up of the Theatre of the Absurd, a summing-up which he thinks has much in common with Wittgenstein's methods in the *Philosophical Investigations*:

---

15. Stanley Cavell, "Ending the Waiting Game," *Must We Mean What We Say?*, p. 116.
16. Ibid., pp. 116–117.

The relativization, devaluation, and criticism of language are also the prevailing trends in contemporary philosophy, as exemplified by Wittgenstein's conviction, in the last phase of his thinking, that the philosopher must endeavour to disentangle thought from the conventions and rules of grammar, which have been mistaken for the rules of logic. . . . By a strict criticism of language, Wittgenstein's followers have declared large categories of statements to be devoid of objective meaning. Wittgenstein's 'word-games' have much in common with the Theatre of the Absurd. (p. 398)

Such comments show that Esslin has very little idea of what Wittgenstein was doing. The characterization of the later philosophy (a term which must not be taken as marking a radical discontinuity with issues discussed in the *Tractatus*) as involving the abandonment of logic is particularly grotesque, since the central questions in Wittgenstein's work were questions of logic to the end. The attack on logic to which Esslin refers is an attack on a certain conception of logic, namely, one which thinks that logic comprises an a priori order prior to all experience. This was one of the pictures that held us captive. Wittgenstein wanted to stress, by contrast, that distinctions between sense and nonsense have their application in the context of the language-games we play. So far from denying that these distinctions exist, he was concerned to show what they come to in various kinds of human discourse. The same would apply to the application of the word 'objective'. What an objective judgment comes to cannot be appreciated in advance of the linguistic context in which it is made. It is difficult to know who Esslin has in mind when he speaks of "Wittgenstein's followers," but when he refers to them approvingly as having "declared large categories of statements to be devoid of objective meaning," it seems that Esslin himself is in the grip of the very picture from which Wittgenstein wants to free us. For Esslin, reality could only be objective if 'objective' meant the same in all contexts. Since 'objective' does not mean the same in every context, there is for Esslin no objective reality. The illusion of objectivity is revealed by the scientific attitude: "The modern scientific attitude, however, rejects the postulate of a wholly coherent and simplified explanation that must account for all the phenomena, purposes and moral rules of the world" (p. 415). Contrary to this, Wittgenstein attacked the scientism which claimed that everything should conform to one paradigm of intelligibility. For Esslin, then, the reason why reality is not objective seems to be because everything is not scientific.

In reply to Esslin's points we need only note that if there are different paradigms of rationality, the religious believer will not think the distinction between the sacred and the profane less objective because all distinctions in human discourse cannot be reduced to this one. Similarly, people who care about the difference between right and wrong will not think that difference invalid because rogues do not live by it. Yet, Esslin thinks these areas of life and others must appear meaningless if language lacks this metaphysical unity. Since the only features of human life, in this context, which are real, would be universal features, features which do not exist, all the descriptions under which human life may fall are accidental and therefore unreal. "That is why, in the analysis of the dramatists of the Absurd ... we have always seen man stripped of the accidental circumstances of social position or historical context, confronted with the basic choices, the basic situations of his existence: man faced with time and therefore waiting" (p. 391). As we have seen, however, if an individual is placed outside all such contexts he becomes something infinitely less than he is, a substanceless point.

Yet, it is from such a point that Esslin believes that hope can be found. He thinks that giving up the search for the world as a unified system is only the first step, but a necessary step:

For if the Theatre of the Absurd presents the world as senseless and lacking a unifying principle, it does so merely in the terms of those philosophies that start from the idea that human thought *can* reduce the totality of the universe to a complete, unified, coherent system. It is only from the point of view of those who cannot bear a world where it is impossible to know why it was created, what part man has been assigned in it, and what constitutes right actions and wrong actions, that a picture of the universe lacking all these clear-cut definitions

appears deprived of sense and sanity, and tragically absurd.
(p. 415)

Since such a unified system is impossible, the features of human
life appear arbitrary and absurd. Yet, these very limitations can
lead to a liberating experience:

> To confront the limits of the human condition is not only
> equivalent to facing up to the philosophical basis of the scien-
> tific attitude, it is also a profound mystical experience. It is
> precisely this experience of the ineffability, the emptiness, the
> nothingness at the basis of the universe that forms the content
> of Eastern as well as Christian mystical experience. (p. 416)

What does this experience amount to? Esslin assures us that

> there is no contradiction between recognizing the limitations
> of man's ability to comprehend all of reality in a single system
> of values and recognizing the mysterious and ineffable one-
> ness, beyond all rational comprehension, that, once experi-
> enced, gives serenity of mind and the strength to face the hu-
> man condition. (p. 418)

Strength and serenity of mind, to be worth anything, cannot
be bought at so cheap a price. Esslin thinks that what he says
has affinities with mysticism. This is a presumptuous claim.
What mystics say is linked to conceptions and traditions of
spirituality. So far from ignoring the detail of human life, their
words can only have force in relation to it. Placing the so-
called illumination beyond all human discourse in the way
Esslin does simply opens the door to obscurantism and an indulgent anti-intellectualism. More strictly, the experience cannot be anything without falling under some description. Placing
the experience beyond all possible descriptions does not locate
what is portrayed in the Theatre of the Absurd. What it lo-
cates is a kind of absurdity with which we are all too familiar
in philosophy — the attempt to say what cannot be said, not
because it is ineffable, but because it does not make sense.

9/INGMAR BERGMAN'S REDUCTIONISM

"A Modern Cosmology of the Spirit"

In *Three Films* BY INGMAR BERGMAN we are told that his theme "in this great trilogy of films is the obsession with God; that strange compelling search for guidance which is, perhaps, doomed by the very essence from which it springs. Bergman calls his treatment of this quest 'a reduction'."[1] Bergman says that 'reduction' is used "in the metaphysical sense of that word" and describes the three films — *Through a Glass Darkly, Winter Light, The Silence* — as "certainty achieved," "certainty unmasked," and "God's silence — the negative impression" (p. 7).

The metaphysical sense of reduction may be commendatory or pejorative. The commendatory use refers to attempts to reduce a phenomenon to more basic terms, terms which reveal its true nature. The pejorative use describes a situation where such an analysis has not worked, where it is claimed that the analysis reduces the character of the original phenomenon to something less than itself. Philosophers differ in specific cases over which kind of reduction we are faced with: Is morality simply enlightened self-interest? Are emotions no more than sensations? Is "God" a product of projection?

The commendatory and pejorative uses of reductionism are not the only alternatives. The classical reductionist claims to show you what a phenomenon really is. The pejorative rejoinder denies this and reasserts what it takes to be the original nature of the phenomenon. But a reductionist analysis may be

---

1. Ingmar Bergman, *Three Films*, trans. Paul Britten Austin (New York: Grove Press, 1970). All references are from this edition. There are some variations from some showings of these films, at least, which are of minor importance, but others are of greater substance. In all cases I quote from the printed text.

showing us, not what a phenomenon has always been, *but what it has become.* For example, it may not be saying that morality has always been a matter of self-interest, but that this is what it has become. Sometimes, it is clear that the analyst knows that he is doing this; that he is tracing the debasement of a concept. At other times, he may not realize that he is doing this. Although in fact he is showing us what morality, love, or belief in God have become, he may think this is what they have always been. He is cut off from the old concepts and his analysis simply acts as testimony to his blindness and their decline.

Where does Bergman stand in this spectrum? Is he in these films showing us what obsession with God has always been, or what it has become? The texts do not answer this one way or the other. Bergman shows us what the obsession is for his characters, but there is no evidence that he is aware of any alternative. In the three films we see a movement from a kind of belief in God to a private individual world of protected sensations: "a modern cosmology of the spirit."

I. THROUGH A GLASS DARKLY: *CERTAINTY ACHIEVED*

Three of the four characters we meet in this film are all, in their different ways, self-centered, finding it difficult to be close to anyone, even within the same family. One of them says: "It's like this. One draws a magic circle around oneself, shutting out everything that hasn't any place in one's own private little game. Every time life smashes the circle the game turns into something grey, tiny, ridiculous. So one draws a new circle, builds up new barriers" (p. 54). Can a belief in God break into these circles without making the game seem ridiculous?

The isolation of Bergman's characters is reflected in the isolation of their location:

The house, strongly marked by its exposed position, stands by itself on a long sandy promontory. Built in two storeys, it is a dark green colour, except where sun and wind have burnished

its timbers to a lighter silky hue. At the back it looks out over
a large wild garden, all run to seed and partly screened from
prying eyes by a high paling. (p. 15)

It is in these surroundings that we meet David, an author of
cheap popular novels, his two children, Minus, a lonely adoles-
cent bothered by an emerging sexuality, and Karin, who is
mentally ill, and her weak indecisive doctor husband, Martin.
Their characters are made manifest in the opening scenes.

We see how Karin's sensuousness bothers Minus and that
she does not hide her nakedness from him. Later he pleads with
her not to make love with Martin where he can hear them,
not to sunbathe scantily clad, and so on. Other tensions exist
between the other characters. Martin has written to David telling him of Karin's illness. There is no hope of recovery in the
long run. It is clear that her father has put his writing before
his daughter. Martin knows this and David knows this himself,
but he is still going away yet again for a period in Yugoslavia.
Furthermore, when the children discuss his writing Minus has
the maturity to see that it does not amount to much. He knows
that his father would like to be a genius and, of course, will
never be one. Nevertheless, he would like to be able to talk
frankly with him, but cannot. After an evening meal the children put on a play about an artist who puts himself before all
things, a thinly disguised allusion to their father's priorities.
After retiring to their bedroom, Karin tells Martin that she
realizes that she is being no wife to him. So every relationship
is fraught with tension and difficulty.

One of the questions Bergman is posing is whether belief in
God can break into such difficulties in such a way as to give
them a sense which is not ridiculous. This question is explored
in the main in his depiction of Karin's illness. We are shown
signs of this illness during the day with which the film opens.
Karin and Minus are walking in the woods. She is able to hear
a cuckoo long before he can, and she comments,

KARIN: ... It's very odd, but since my illness my hearing has
become so sensitive. Maybe it was the electroshocks, I can't
say. Sudden loud noises send me out of my wits.
... They hasten their footsteps. Around them the forest

grows darker. Somewhere in the distance thunder rumbles.
Karin stops.

KARIN: Oh, no, no, no.   No.
MINUS (*softly*): What is it?
KARIN: No, no. Nothing.
MINUS: Sure?
KARIN: No, nothing. Don't be scared. It's nothing. (*Pause*) Can
    you hear the thunder . . . ?
MINUS: Sure. (pp. 18-19)

Here, something seems to be trying to break into Karin's
world, but it is something alien, threatening. Yet, it is seen by
her as a higher reality, one which could give sense to her life.
All you have to do is to listen, open yourself up to it. There
are echoes in this scene of the occult: a belief in a somewhere
else, strange, fascinating, more real than anything we know.
When the circle is grey and boring how attractive is the prospect of an escape into a region of fantasy. But, on this occasion,
normality reasserts itself, familiar descriptions return: "No,
nothing. Don't be scared. It's nothing. (*Pause*) Can you hear
the thunder . . . ?" — "Sure."

The return of normality does not solve Bergman's problem,
since that very normality in his characters is that which cries
out for a sense to redeem it. Let us now look at how an attempt
is made to let sense break in. We can see this in terms of the
events during the first night. Neither Minus nor David can
sleep. The boy goes off to a fisherman's hut while his father
tries to work on his novel. Shortly before sunrise "*Karin, who
has been sleeping beside her husband awakes abruptly, all ears,
as if someone were calling her*" (p. 31). She makes her way to
a first-floor room:

*In the hall Karin hesitates, but then goes into the room which
looks out toward the sunrise. She tries to close the door behind
her but the frame has warped and the lock is broken.*
*Apart from an old Windsor chair and a little nursery table,
this room is void of furniture. The floor, which once con-
sisted of clean-scrubbed boards, has been partially ripped up
and the floorboards are propped against the wall. What immediately strikes the eye in this room, however, is its wallpaper. Green in colour, it is really supposed to represent leaves*

*in various shades, tones and tinges. In some spots the colour
has faded completely and the pattern appears only very faint
and grey; but in corners and behind the pictures the foliage is
still strong and leafy. In the wall to the right of the window
is a narrow door, also covered with wallpaper, above which a
patch of damp has exploded and given birth to a laughing
moon-face with one dud eye, a gaping mouth and a high
potato nose. To the left of the window, over the whole width
of one strip, the pattern of leaves has been ripped away, and
behind it a stiff brownish composition with fading golden
edges has come into view.*

*Karin has come to a halt in the middle of the room; her pos-
ture is one of petrified attentiveness, as if expecting to hear
someone speak to her. She has let go of her dressing-gown
and holds her hand out motionlessly before her; her head is
turned to one side and her gaze is fixed on the right-hand wall.
Suddenly, small flames of fire are alight in the heavy petals of
the wallpaper, a convulsive puff of wind comes from the sea
and the house sighs like an old ship with its masts and rigging.
The disc of the sun comes rolling out of the grey ocean swell
and little orange tongues of fire flicker over the wallpaper's
leafy designs.*

*Karin gives a sigh, breathes deeply; a sound, as of repressed
singing or whispering, stirs in her throat. Her face swells and
darkens and her eyes become glazed, unaware.*

Slowly, she sinks down on her knees, legs wide apart.
(pp. 32-33)

This scene in the film is a powerful one, but it is important
to be clear where its power lies. Her repressed singing or
whispering is parasitic for its force on what a real song might
say or what secret might be conveyed in a whisper. She wants
her condition to be informed by something. She awaits a message. Yet, if we were asked what that message might be, we
could give no clear answer. Bergman is depicting the inarticulate longing of madness. Yet, he is trading on wider associations.
Karin, though mad, expresses a view of religion uncomfortably
close to the conceptions of many who are not mad. The spiritual is equated with the uncanny. Things of the spirit become
unusual spirits. If we ask what bearing these religious phenomena have on human life, we can see that they have a bearing

similar to Karin's experience: that of an inarticulate something which gets its suggestion of profundity from half-expressed echoes of what can be genuine in other circumstances. It is not too much to say that Bergman's film is, to a great extent, a celebration of the inarticulate in a realm which has pretensions to be a realm of the spirit. This is a bold claim which has to be substantiated.

While these traumatic events are happening to Karin, her father is trying to work on his novel. Here, too, the inarticulate dominates. This is brought out quite humorously:

DAVID *(reads)*: She came toward him, panting with expectation scarlet-faced in the keen wind... *(sighs)* Oh my God, oh my God.
He thrusts his spectacles up on his brow and hides his grey face in his hands. But after a few moments he resumes work.
DAVID *(reads)*: She came toward him, panting with expectation...
He runs a long thin line through the rest of the sentence, and contemplates his work. Then he strikes out all the rest too.
DAVID: She came running toward him, her face scarlet in the keen wind...
He shakes his head and leans forward over his sheets of paper, and in capital letters, in red ink, writes the following: SHE CAME RUNNING TOWARD HIM. Then he gives a sigh, shakes his head, runs a thick line through what he has written in capital letters and resolutely writes: "They met on the beach." (pp. 33-34)

Suddenly, Karin appears. He puts her to sleep on his own bed and goes to collect in nets with Minus. As soon as they have gone Karin wakes up and, rummaging in her father's desk, discovers his notebook. There she reads:

KARIN: "Her illness is hopeless, with occasional improvements. I have long suspected it, but the certainty, even so, is almost unbearable. To my horror, I note my own curiosity. The impulse to register its course, to note concisely her gradual dissolution. To make use of her." (p. 35)

In all the scenes we have so far, the inarticulate predominates. In Karin it appears in her longing in madness for some secret message. Minus can't make sense of the way his desires are developing. David does not know what he wants to say in his work or to his children. The relationship between Karin and Martin is no exception. Although she can tell him how her father is using her, she shrinks from his timid comforting touch.

What is to break in on these situations? What is to penetrate these circles? Bergman's answer to this question is shown in the events of the second day. David and Martin go to town to do some shopping. Having gone too far in teasing Minus about his interest in sex, Karin promises to take him into her confidence. She takes him to the first-floor room:

KARIN: D'you know what — I can walk straight through this wall.

MINUS (*doesn't reply*).

KARIN: Can't imagine how it's done. Early this morning I was woken by a voice calling me, quite definitely calling. I got up and came to this room. Just at sunrise, and inside me a tremendous longing, a tremendous power. One day some-one called to me from behind the wallpaper, and I looked inside the cupboard, but it was empty. The voice went on calling me, so I pressed myself against the wall and it opened up like a lot of leaves *and there I was inside!*

Breaking off, she smiles quickly and mockingly.

MINUS: What is it?

KARIN: You think I'm making it up?

MINUS (*shakes his head*).

Again she runs her hand over the wallpaper, seems suddenly absent. Minus is very tense, but doesn't dare disturb the sudden silence.

KARIN: I come into a big room, quite still and silent, people are moving about and someone speaks to me and I understand. It's so lovely. I feel so safe. Some of the faces are radiant with light.

All are waiting for him who is to come, but no one worries. They say I can be with them when it happens.

MINUS: Why are you crying?

KARIN: No, it's nothing dangerous. But you see, Minus, some-times I'm overcome with such a terrible longing. I long for that moment when the door will open and all faces are turned towards him who's to come.

MINUS: Who is it, who's coming?

KARIN: I don't know, no one has said anything definite, but I believe God is going to reveal himself to us. And he'll come in to us through that door. *(Pause)* Everyone's so calm — and so gentle. And they're waiting. And their love... LOVE... (p. 42)

Love is supposed to be the answer in some sense, but, then, no one has said anything definite. Neither has Bergman. In this whole scene, the divine is characterized, not by its bearing on human life, but by something which should be traceable to a strange source. Karin's other world has little to do with the wise recognition that the spiritual, while not being of the world, must work in it. On the contrary, if she could enter her world it would cut her off from the ordinary world she now inhabits. What this new world has to offer neither she nor its alleged inhabitants can say. Despite the fact that they wait serenely, unlike Vladimir and Estragon, the people in this mysterious room too wait for something they know not what.

Unlike Karin, who longs for something she has not got, David is supposed to have a firm faith. But when Bergman tells us what it is, his condition seems scarcely more articulate than Karin's. Returning from their shopping, Martin tells David that there is no truth in his books or in him. He accuses him of using Karin: "You're empty and clever and now you think you'll fill your emptiness with Karin's extinction. The only thing I don't understand is how you fancy you can mix God up in all this. He must be more inscrutable than ever" (p. 46).

This is to be Bergman's question: how *does* God get mixed up in all this? Can we find an answer in David's confession to Martin? At first he gives an ironic answer in suggesting that everything can be solved by good intentions.

DAVID: The main thing is to believe in one's own good intentions. Then everything solves itself, as if by magic. Provided you go through the correct motions.

When Martin asks whether David is referring to him, he replies, "Shouldn't dare... I assure you my irony is mostly directed against myself." So David, at least, does not believe in the magical efficacy of good intentions. But then the conversation continues:

MARTIN: But you can find consolation in your religion.
DAVID: Yes.
MARTIN: And inscrutable grace.
DAVID: Yes.
MARTIN: It *is* inscrutable? (p. 47)

Clearly, what we are now to hear about religion and inscrutable grace is meant to be a contrast to the magic of good intentions. What we are given is in fact another brand of magic:

DAVID: I'll tell you something. Down there in Switzerland I decided to kill myself. I'd hired a small car and found a precipice. As I drove out there I was quite calm. It was a very lonely road, no traffic. And it was evening; down in the valley it was already dark. I was empty, without fear, remorse or expectation. So I went straight for the precipice. As I pressed the accelerator down, the engine stalled; the gear stopped me dead. The car slid a few yards on the loose gravel surface, then hung there with its front wheels over the edge. I dragged myself out, trembling all over; had to sit down under the cliff on the other side of the road. And there I sat, gasping for breath, for several hours.
MARTIN: What are you telling me all this for?
DAVID: I want to tell you I no longer have any façades to keep up. Truth requires no catastrophes. I can see myself.
MARTIN: This hasn't anything to do with Karin.
DAVID: Yes, I think it has.
MARTIN: I don't understand.
DAVID: Out of my emptiness something was born which I hardly dare touch or give a name to. A love. *(Pause)* For Karin and Minus. And you. (p. 47)

But this love is as magical as the good intentions he spoke of. What purchase does it have in his relationship with the other characters? Very little. It is as if David thinks that the love born in a moment of supreme danger is something which can be given complete, all at once. This is a romantic concept of love which has little in common with that love which is patient, suffers long, and is kind. After all, we have already been told that he is off to Yugoslavia — the very thing he knows distresses his children most. He is deserting them as he deserted their mother in her need. So what bearing has the new-found love on this elementary lack of consideration? We are given no answer. The love is as magical as the intentions; a short-cut which tries to avoid working through the difficulties. Again, the inarticulate predominates.

Similar conclusions can be reached about the way in which reality is supposed to burst in on Minus's adolescence. While David and Martin are away, Minus and Karin have to take refuge from heavy rain. He finds her eventually in an old wreck:

> *Suddenly she has clasped him tight and he falls headlong on top of her, struggles to get free, but can't, sinks more deeply into her. He catches a glimpse of naked skin, an odour of sea-weed, rotten wood, the sea bottom. She holds him tight to her with her arms and legs, but her face is averted, her mouth tightly closed.*
> *Then the rain begins thudding on the deck. Slowly, he frees himself and lifts his head. He sits beside her, incapable of movement, choked by tears.* (p. 49)

Gradually he turns to Karin, but he can get little response from her. As she slowly recovers consciousness she tells Minus she is ill and pleads for his help. He runs back to the house to get her some water:

> *Minus rushes into his room and throws himself on his knees on the floor and clasps his hands, bends his head and presses his hands to his lips.*
> MINUS (whispering): God . . . God . . . help us!
> *. . . Again and again he calls on God. At length, exhausted, he falls silent. Stands still a few moments, then tears a couple of blankets off his bed and goes out into the hall, where he rolls them up in a raincoat. Then he flings on his oilskins and hurries back toward the wreck.*
> *Karin is on all fours beneath the hatch, rocking to and fro, feeling very sick; opens her mouth convulsively, as if yawning; now and then a whimpering sound forces itself out of her throat.* (p. 50)

Minus manages to wrap her in blankets. He manages to soothe her down as he rocks her in his arms. There they stay until they hear the motorboat signaling the return of David and Martin.

What are we to make of Minus's call to God in his distress? Not much, I think. Any name might have come to his lips. Even if we do say the call is significant, what is sought is again some kind of magical intervention, some shortcut, which will make everything all right. Yet, according to Bergman's film commentary, the whole incident has brought about a whole change of perspective for Minus:

> *Minus is sitting somewhere in eternity with his sick sister in his arms. He is empty, exhausted, frozen. Reality, as he has known it until now, has been shattered, ceased to exist. Neither in his dreams nor his fantasies has he known anything to correspond to this moment of weightlessness and grief. His mind has forced its way through the membrane of merciful ignorance. From this moment on his senses will change and harden, his receptivity will become sharpened, as he goes from the make-believe world of innocence to the torment of insight. The world of contingency and chance has been transformed into a universe of law. (p. 51)*

It must be said that these lavish words must be put on the same level as the good intentions, instant awareness of love, and the calling on God in a panic. They are words which want to convey an instant breakthrough in awareness in Minus, but there is nothing in the development of the character which merits these words. When Minus refers to these incidents in the last conversation with his father in the film things are no clearer:

MINUS: As I was sitting in the wreck down there, holding Karin, reality burst in pieces for me. D'you understand what I mean?

DAVID: I understand.

MINUS: Reality burst and I fell out. It's like in a dream, though real. Anything can happen — *anything* Daddy!

DAVID: Yes, I know.

MINUS: I'm so terrified I could scream. (pp. 59-60)

David says he understands Minus, but do we? All right, he recognizes that anything may happen and this terrifies him. But what bearing is this to have on his life? A Simone Weil reflecting on this fact reaches conclusions very different from someone who concludes that in that case he'd better grab his chances while he can. How is the realization to be worked out in Minus? Bergman's words are, for this purpose, as inscrutable as the inscrutable grace Martin accuses David of turning to for consolation.

We have seen, in fact, how the love, which is supposed to inform the predicaments Bergman depicts, is as inarticulate as the characters' understanding of these predicaments. I said that in these matters Bergman indulges in a celebration. This is because often in this film the prevalence of the inarticulate is the expression of his own belief that nothing can be said here, that God cannot get mixed up in human suffering in a way which places it under an illuminating aspect. At the end of the film David does try to make a positive statement of a more constructive kind, but it is unsatisfactory. From this point, to the end of the film, we can see Bergman's unsuccessful attempt to cast light on the relation between man's obsession with God and the everyday world he must live in.

When Martin and David return, Minus calls them to help Karin. They send for an ambulance helicopter. She tells them that the voices which come to her have made her do terrible things. She wants to stay in hospital until she is cured: "Nobody can live in two worlds. You have to choose" (p. 52). Isn't this what Bergman is expressing in this film, whether he intends to or not? He too cannot portray any relation between the two worlds, the divine and the human. Like Karin, he could say, "I can't make any sense of it" (p. 53). There is little doubt about which of these worlds is the unreal one. The other world, despite being the product of Karin's madness, is one we shall meet again in Bergman's other films. What he seems to be saying at times is that religion is a kind of evil madness. This is brought out in the climax of Karin's illness. Having eluded everyone she is found in the first-floor room, her face pressed to the wallpaper, speaking secretively. She has been told that it won't be long now; the god is about to come. Martin tries to reason with her: "You're wrong Karin. Nothing is happening in there. (*Pause*) Karin! No god is coming out of that door." She is angry with him for disturbing the gravity of the occasion. Martin tires, realizing the futility of his protests. Her longing is about to be fulfilled. But who is the god that will come? I quote the scene in full:

KARIN (*in a low voice*): They say he's in the next room and they can hear his voice. (*Even lower*) Martin, dearest, forgive me for being so nasty just now. But can't you kneel down too, and clasp your hands, here, beside me? It looks so demonstrative and odd, you sitting there in that chair. I know you don't believe; but for my sake, Martin.

Martin shakes his head. He tries to say something but he can't. In the end he slips down on the floor beside his wife and leans his head against her shoulder.

MARTIN: Karin, dearest, dearest, dearest.

Gently, as if disturbed and hurt by his sudden and as it were indecent intervention, she draws away. He reaches out his hand, but she doesn't take it.

Now the engines of the helicopter can be heard, the sound grows swiftly until within a few moments it is a tremendous roar, shaking the whole house. As the machine passes close above the roof there is a brief glimpse of it through the window, a gigantic dark insect.

The windowpanes rattle and Karin slowly gets up. The door in the wallpaper opens wide against the darkness of the cupboard.

She stands tense, radiant with expectancy. Then her countenance changes. She seems to see something coming out of the cupboard, something that swiftly approaches her. Shrinks away. Runs several steps backwards. Flattens herself against the wall. Presses her hands between her legs. A gurgling scream of horror forces itself out of her throat. With all her force she flings herself at Martin, who falls over and loses his glasses. As she clings to him the animal-like cry forces itself again and again out of her mouth.

Martin has grasped hold of her, but she tears herself away. Rushing out of the door she meets David. He, too, tries to catch her. But she is suddenly endowed with immense, super-

human strength.

Rushing for the stairs, she takes a couple of steps down but stops.

At the bottom stands Minus, looking up at her. She sinks down on the step and arches herself with her hands. David throws himself down beside her, clasps her tight.

The next moment Martin arrives. In his right hand he has his hypodermic needle.

MARTIN: Hold her legs.

This in a suddenly calm tone to Minus, who obeys, flinging himself over the violently kicking feet.

Martin draws aside her skirt, rubs the outside of her thigh with a wad of cotton, inserts the needle.

Karin flings herself about in convulsive jerks. Martin protects her head with both his hands. David, mumbling inaudible words, embraces her. Gradually the attack subsides and she becomes still.

Martin fetches water in a cup. She drinks thirstily. Then sits up and pulls her skirt down over her knees, straightening her hair.

KARIN: I was frightened.

A few moments she is silent, takes the cup from Martin and swallows another gulp.

KARIN: The door opened. But the god who came out was a spider. He had six legs and moved very fast across the floor.

She is shaken by terror and disgust as she speaks. By an effort of will she controls herself.

KARIN: He came up to me and I saw his face, a loathsome evil face. And he clambered up onto me and tried to force himself into me. But I protected myself. All the time I saw his eyes. They were cold and calm. When he couldn't force himself into me, he climbed quickly up onto my breast and my face and went on up the wall.

Again she is silent. Martin takes the cup from her hand and unscrews his hypodermic needle. She meets Minus's gaze but no longer recognizes him.

KARIN: I've seen God.

This she says with complete calm, but beneath the surface trembles a new and breathless horror whose swiftly growing roots are entangling themselves around her soul. (pp. 57-59)

This, then, is the result of trying to marry two worlds, of

trying to establish a relation between what belongs to man and what belongs to God. After Karin has been taken away, Minus expresses his rejection of this spider god, the conception of the supernatural as the uncanny and unknown beyond human life.

MINUS: I can't live with this new thing, Daddy.
DAVID: Yes, you can. But you must have something to hold on to.
MINUS: And what could that be? A god? A spider god like Karin's? Or an invisible potentate somewhere in the dark? No. It's no good.
Silence.
MINUS: No, Daddy, it's no good. God doesn't exist in my world. (p. 60)

Here we have confirmation of the fact that although the spider god is a product of Karin's madness, Bergman is questioning the whole notion of a god who dwells in some other world conceived by analogy with this one; a god who may be strange but nevertheless a god who is an object among objects, a creature among creatures, a something in the dark. If this is the only bearing religion has on life, it is little more than the product of superstitious fear, the desire for magical solutions and trivial curiosity. Religion is little more than the occult. Is this all religion can be?

It appears that David has more to offer, something to hold on to even in face of the traumas they have witnessed. He has destroyed his manuscript after witnessing the last stages of Karin's illness and we are told that as he watches her depart he is free from self-pity for the first time. But these are indications of a change of attitude, nothing more.

David's faith is expounded in his last conversation with Minus with which the film ends. David tries to show what we can mean by God if he is to be more than a something in the dark. The trouble is that his words, like those we have met at other points throughout the film, seek a magical solution, a shortcut which solves everything all at once. Nevertheless, the beginning of David's conversation with Minus could have been promising:

MINUS (*full of anxiety*): Give me some proof of God.
Silence.
MINUS: You can't.
DAVID: Yes I can. But you must listen carefully to what I'm
    saying, Minus.
MINUS: That's just what I need, to listen.
DAVID: It's written: *God is love.*
MINUS: For me that's just words and nonsense.
DAVID: Wait a moment and don't interrupt. (p. 60)

To show that God is real is to show that a certain kind of
love is real. The 'is' in 'God is love' is not an 'is' of predica-
tion, but an 'is' of identity. When we learn the use of the word
'love' in certain contexts, we learn one use of the word 'God' at
the same time. David says that his hopes lie "in the knowledge
that love exists as something real in the world of men" (p. 60).
But to this Minus makes a crucial response: "Of course it's a
special sort of love you're referring to." Some philosophers have
objected to saying that God and love can be identified by arguing that this turns 'God is love' into the empty tautology, 'Love
is love'. This would be true if divine love were identified with
any kind of love. Minus, it seems, half recognizes this, and asks
what kind of love David is referring to. But in David's answer
Bergman ducks the issue:

MINUS: Of course it's a special sort of love you're referring to.
DAVID: *Every* sort of love, Minus! The highest and the lowest,
    the poorest and the richest, the most ridiculous and the
    most sublime. The obsessive and the banal. All sorts of love.
MINUS (*silent*): Longing for love.
DAVID: Longing and denial. Disbelieving and being consoled.
MINUS: So love is the proof?
DAVID: We can't know whether love proves God's existence or
    whether love is itself God. After all, it doesn't make very
    much difference.
MINUS: For you God and love are one and the same phenom-
    enon.
DAVID: I let my emptiness, my dirty hopelessness, rest in that
    thought, yes. (*Falls silent*).
MINUS: Tell me, Daddy.
DAVID: Suddenly the emptiness turns into wealth, and hope-

lessness into life. It's like a pardon, Minus. From a sentence of death. (pp. 60-61)

David identifies the love of God with *any* kind of love — the highest and the lowest. Once he does this, he cannot show how divine love can bring salvation to a world of human love and hate since he has identified divine love with human love. Minus's response is equally unsatisfactory: "Your words are terribly unreal, Daddy, but I see you mean what you say. And it makes me tremble all over" (p. 61). This will not do. If the words are unreal, how can they have this so-called profound effect? Here we are back in the realm of good intentions. The same is true when David assures Minus that what he has said can help Karin in her predicament:

MINUS: Can it help her?
DAVID: I think so. (p. 61)

How are the words less unreal? If we have got rid of the spider god in the dark, what we are offered is little more than whistling in the dark.

The film ends with a repetition of these basic weaknesses in Minus's words after his father goes to prepare a meal: "Daddy spoke to me!" No doubt the conversation we have witnessed is an advance in their relationship. At least David has said something. But this is a minimal advance, since what he has said are the unreal words.

In *Through a Glass Darkly* Bergman can only offer a conception of another world which is occult in character. Out of this world comes the spider god which he wants, rightly, to be rid of. The alternative David offers is to identify God with love. This is the certainty which is supposed to be achieved in the film. But what kind of certainty is it? Is it a vague hope in some kind of ultimate compensation, a conviction that somehow everything will be all right? Further, God is identified with any kind of love. That being so, how can divine love say anything in face of the deficiencies and ambiguities of human love since it has been identified with these? The words which David offers us are, Minus tells us, unreal words. Is he right? Perhaps the hope for divine compensation for the ills that beset us is unreal. Perhaps even human love is not what it seems. If divine love can be reduced to any kind of human love, can human love itself be reduced to something else? Having called *Through a Glass Darkly* "certainty achieved," it is significant that Bergman describes the second film in his trilogy, *Winter Light*, as "certainty unmasked."

II. WINTER LIGHT: *CERTAINTY UNMASKED*

In Bergman's second film we are confronted more directly with the question of whether religious faith can speak to the problems of men and women. As Tomas Eriksson celebrates morning communion everything about the church building and the congregation seems to be a sign of decay and decline. All this is in marked contrast to the words he utters feverishly, suffering from influenza. The words seem empty to him:

> TOMAS (*continues*): He is the lamb of our Passover, sacrificed for us, who beareth all the world's sins, even unto death. And even as He hath overcome death and risen again and liveth for ever, so shall we and all who put their trust in Him, through Him overcome sin and death and inherit eternal life.
>
> TOMAS (*listens*): *This silence, colourless, empty—as in a dream.* Wherefore we, with Thy faithful at all times and with all the heavenly host, praise Thy name and sing in supplication. (p. 66)

But do these words speak to the faithful at all times? Despite the fact that there are two hundred and sixty-seven souls in his parish, only nine have turned up for morning communion. None of them seem able to participate in the right spirit. An old lady takes the bread and wine greedily. She is a regular communicant. Jonas Persson, a thirty-five year old fisherman and carpenter, seems preoccupied throughout. Märta Lundberg, a thirty-three year old schoolmistress, is more interested in the vicar than in the sacrament.

Jonas Persson and his wife want to see the vicar. She is concerned with her husband's obsession with the Chinese. He has read that they are brought up to hate, that they'll have atom

bombs soon, and that they'd be prepared to die. Tomas can't
say anything to him. The obsession is crazy, but Jonas knows
that the vicar can't tell him anything.

> TOMAS: We live our simple daily lives. And then some terrible
> piece of information forces itself into our secure, safe
> world. It's more than we can bear. The whole state of af-
> fairs is so overwhelming, God becomes so remote.
> *Jonas, smiling, shakes his head. He seems to pity them.*
> MRS. PERSSON (*dubiously*): Yes, yes.
> TOMAS: I feel so helpless. I don't know what to say. I under-
> stand your fear, God, how I understand it! But we must
> go on living.
> JONAS: Why must we go on living?
> TOMAS: Because we must. We have a responsibility.
> JONAS: You aren't well, Vicar, and I shouldn't sit here talking.
> Anyway we won't get anywhere.
> TOMAS (*anxiously*): Yes! Let's talk to each other. Let's say
> whatever comes into our heads.
> *The fisherman looks at the vicar in astonishment, then slowly
> shakes his head. The pitying smile returns.* (p. 74)

No wonder Jonas is astonished. Having reluctantly come to
hear what the vicar has to say, he hears the suggestion that they
should say anything that comes into their heads. Although
Tomas realizes that Jonas is in a desperate state he knows that
he has talked a lot of drivel. Later when Märta Lundberg asks
him what is wrong he replies, "God's silence." For her, there
is no problem. She wants to consummate their affair in marriage, although she knows that he does not love her and that he
knows she does not believe in God. She has little patience with
his anguish: "Sometimes I think you're the limit! God's silence,
God doesn't speak. God hasn't ever spoken, because he doesn't
exist. It's all so unusually, horribly simple" (p. 78).

But does Bergman simply present a choice between a God
who has temporarily ceased to speak and the belief that God
has never spoken? I think not. He is wanting to say that there
is a senselessness which is integral to religious faith. He makes
the church architecture express this. After seeing the Perssons
depart Tomas "*goes out into the church, stands absent-minded-*

ly in front of the altar: Christ on the cross, between God's knees. God himself has black hair and a brown beard and eyebrows raised as if in surprise" (p. 75). Tomas calls it a ridiculous image. Not even God can understand what is going on on the cross. Further tensions are expressed in the crucifix which hangs opposite the vestry window:

> *...It is a crude, roughly carved image of the suffering Christ, ineptly made. The mouth opens in a scream, the arms are grotesquely twisted, the hands convulsively clutch the nails, the brow is bloody beneath the thorns, and the body arches outwards, as if trying to tear itself away from the wood. The image smells of fungus, moldy timber. Its paint is flaking off in long strips.* (p. 79)

Not only does God not understand what is happening to Christ, Christ does not understand what is happening to himself. It seems as if he wants to escape from his fate. It is not simply that the crucifix is ineptly made. Bergman is suggesting that there is an ineptitude in what it expresses. The mold and decay are not only in the image; they are in the faith itself. Märta has no doubt about the matter: "I have never believed in your faith. Chiefly, of course, because I've never been tormented by religious temptation. I grew up in a non-Christian family, full of warmth and kindness and loyalty – and joy. God and Christ didn't exist, except as vague notions. And when I came into contact with your faith, it seemed to me obscure and neurotic, in some way cruelly overcharged with emotion, primitive" (p. 81).

Bergman's reductionism begins to take a definite form. Religious faith is the product of the neurotic and unloving elements of life. Where normal love and warmth prevail, there is no opportunity for religion to take root. In his heart, Tomas feels the emptiness too.

Tomas has asked Jonas Persson to return so that he may talk to him again. He tries to palm him off with small talk, but the only time Jonas shows any interest is when Tomas tells him that he has had no reason for living since the death of his wife. Jonas can see no reason for living either, so he waits to hear what Tomas has received from religion as sustenance. What he hears astounds him. Tomas confesses that his religion never spoke to the realities of life: "I and my God lived in one world, a specially arranged world, where everything made sense. All around were the agonies of real life. But I didn't see them. I turned my gaze toward my God" (p. 84). The God to which he turns is a god of compensation who sees that everything works out in the end: "An improbable, entirely private, fatherly god. Who loved mankind, of course, but most of all me. . . . A god who guaranteed me every imaginable security. Against fear of death. Against fear of life. A god I'd suggested myself into believing in" (pp. 84-85). When the world ceases to smile on us, it is tempting to create a God who does. Yet, if we have the courage to face such a belief with human suffering, the ugliness of our conceptions becomes apparent: "Every time I confronted God with the reality I saw, he became ugly, revolting, a spider god — a monster" (p. 85). Here is a direct quote from *Through a Glass Darkly*.

Listening to the vicar Jonas becomes more and more agitated and tries to leave more than once. But Tomas knows the man is on the brink of suicide. He decides to be even more frank in his confession:

TOMAS: Well, and what if God doesn't exist? What difference does it make?

JONAS *(looks towards the door)*.

TOMAS: Life becomes something we can understand. What a relief! And death — extinction, dissolution of body and soul. People's cruelty, their loneliness, their fear — everything becomes self-evident — transparent. Suffering is incomprehensible, so it needn't be explained. The stars out in space, worlds, heavens, all have given birth to themselves and to each other. There isn't any creator, no one who holds it all together, no immeasureable thought to make one's head spin. . . .

You must live, Jonas. Summer's on the way. After all, the darkness won't last for ever. You've got your strawberry beds, haven't you, and your flowering jasmine. What perfume! Long hot days. It's the earthly paradise, Jonas. It's something to live for!

JONAS *(looks at the wall)*.

TOMAS: We'll see a lot of each other, you and I. We'll become good friends, and talk to each other about this dark day. We've given gifts to each other, haven't we? You've given me your fear and I've given you a god I've killed.

JONAS *(looks away)*.

TOMAS: I don't feel well, I've got a fever. Everything's swaying about. I . . . I can't collect my thoughts. I'm ill. The fact is, I'm in a wretched state.

He lays his arms on the table and supports his forehead on his hands. Shaken by feverish chills, he moans faintly, the sweat breaks out on his forehead and temples and on his hands. Gradually the attack subsides. He becomes quieter. When he looks up Jonas has vanished. (pp. 86-87)

Tomas drags himself to the window to see if he can see any sign of Jonas:

No car, no traces. Not a sound. The snow falls softly and steadily. God's silence, Christ's twisted face, the blood on the brow and hands, the soundless shriek behind the bared teeth. God's silence.

TOMAS *(moaning)*: God, my God, why have you abandoned me? (p. 87)

But the God whom he feels abandoned by is, from all the evidence we have, the God of compensation. The God who will fix everything. He throws himself full-length on the floor of the chancel, but eventually raises himself on the palms of his hands:

TOMAS: No. *(Pause)* God does not exist any more. . . . I'm free now. At last, free. (p. 87)

At most his freedom is negative; freedom from the spider-god. As he and Märta prepare to go to an afternoon service one of his parishioners brings the news that Jonas has killed himself with his shotgun. On the way to the service they stop for some medicine at Märta's schoolhouse. They meet a young lad whose elder brother attends confirmation classes, but who does not attend himself. The boy wants to be a spaceman when he grows up. Tomas smiles suddenly: "Sure. I understand" (p. 91).

The explorations of coming generations will not be religious in character. But Tomas does not belong to that generation. What is his new-found freedom supposed to be? Not a freedom to love Märta. On the contrary, he tells her that he is completely fed up with her. For all his talk of suffering, hers irritates him: "You force me to occupy myself with your physical condition, your bad stomach, your eczemas, your periods, your frost-bitten cheek. Once and for all I must get out of all this rubbish, this junkheap of idiotic circumstances. I'm sick and tired of the whole thing, of everything to do with you" (p. 94). But Märta does not believe he has attained any kind of freedom: "Oh no, you won't be able to manage. You'll go under, dearest Tomas. Nothing can save you. You'll hate the life out of yourself" (p. 95).

When Tomas and Märta break the news of her husband's death to Mrs. Persson on their way to the church, her reaction is simply to say, "So, I'm alone then." She does not want the vicar to read from the Bible. Bergman's suggestion is that such a reading would hold out hopes of false consolations. But it is such consolation that Tomas craves for. As they continue their journey he tells Märta of a nightmare he had as a boy:

> TOMAS: One evening when I was a boy I woke up in a terrible state of fright. . . . I got out of bed, ran round all the rooms looking for Father. But the house was empty. I shouted and screamed, but no one answered. So I dressed as well as I could and ran down to the shore, all the time screaming and crying for Father. . . . I'd been left without Father and Mother in a completely dead world. I was sick with terror. Father sat up and watched over me all night.
> MARTA (*absent-mindedly*): What a nice father!
> TOMAS: Father and Mother wanted me to become a parson (*pause*) and I did as they wished. (p. 98)

If we needed further confirmation of Tomas's God of consolation and compensation, we have it here. He wanted his father to see that nothing would go wrong. When his father died he invented a god who would see that nothing would go wrong. But the nightmare has become reality. His human father is dead and the heavenly one does not exist. In fact, on

Bergman's view, if we understood the passion of Christ correctly, this is what it's trying to tell us. This view is put to Tomas by Algot Frövik, who is lighting the lamps in the chancel when Tomas and Märta arrive at the church. He had wanted to discuss difficulties he felt about the Passion that morning, but now he has an opportunity. He does not think the actual torture should be emphasized, since many may have suffered greater physical pain than Christ. The point of the Passion is "to understand that no one has understood you. To be abandoned when one really needs someone to rely on. A terrible suffering" (p. 101). This is what happened to Christ.

> ALGOT: ... When Christ had been nailed up on the cross and hung there in his torments, he cried out: "God, my God, why hast thou forsaken me." He cried out as loud as he possibly could. He thought his Father in Heaven had abandoned him. He believed everything he'd been preaching was a lie. The moments before he died Christ was seized with a great doubt. Surely that must have been his most monstrous suffering of all? I mean God's silence. Isn't that true, Vicar?
>
> TOMAS: Yes, yes. *(Nods, averting his face).* (p. 101)

Bergman has no other conception of the Passion to offer. It is the revelation of a mistake, the mistake of thinking that there is a compensating God. On this view, if there are no theodicies, nothing makes sense. The God to which David urged Minus to turn in *Through a Glass Darkly* was a God of love who would see that things would go well. This was a certainty achieved, but that certainty is now unmasked. No such compensations exist.

Apart from Algot only Märta and Blom, the organist, are in the church. They do not think there will be a service and are surprised when Tomas decides to hold one. It may be tempting to think that Tomas goes through the old routine hoping sense will return to it, but we have been given no sense which could return. Surely, in the light of all we have seen and heard, the last words of the film are words of heavy irony:

During the hymn Tomas goes up to the altar, kneels, rises,

turns a pale and anxiety-filled face to his congregation.
TOMAS: Holy, holy, holy, Lord God Almighty. All the earth
    is full of his glory ... (p.104)

Despite all the senselessness in his life, however, we may feel
that at least one thing was real in Tomas's life — his wife's love.
But Blom tells Märta that although Tomas loved his wife like
a lunatic, she "hadn't a genuine feeling in her own body, not
an honest thought. That's what you can call love, if you like!
Jesus! But it put an end to the vicar, it did. And now he's done
for" (p. 102). He goes on, "Listen, Märta. That's how it was
with *that* love. (*Quotes*): 'God is love, and love is God. Love
is the proof of God's existence. Love exists as something real
in the world of men and women.' I know the jargon, as you
can hear" (p. 103). Here we have the second reference to
Through a Glass Darkly. There, David had rejected the god
of the occult, the spider god, in favor of a God of love. Yet,
this god, if thought of as a compensating god, is just as unreal.
Minus was right — the words *are* unreal. But David had reduced divine reality to *any* kind of love, believing that "love
exists as something real in the world of men and women." This
is Tomas's jargon. But, Blom tells us, Tomas has "got as much
knowledge of human nature as my old goloshes." Could it be
that a further reduction awaits us; that when we look from
divine love to human love, human love too turns out to be
something other than it seems? That is what Bergman explores
in the final film in his trilogy.

III. THE SILENCE: *GOD'S SILENCE—*
THE NEGATIVE IMPRESSION

It has already been suggested in *Winter Light* that there may
be something sham in saying "love exists as something real in the
world of men and women." The confidence with which this
remark has been made in *Through a Glass Darkly* has retreated
somewhat in the second film. In *The Silence* it retreats even
further. The question here is what form any genuine love *can*
take. Things are seldom what they seem to be on the surface.
We see all this quite soon in the film. Two sisters, Anna and

Ester, are travelling with Johan, Anna's ten year old son, by train in a foreign country. The initial impression we have of the sisters, one sensual and the other prim, is determined by the physical postures in the stifling heat on the night express:

> Anna, sweating and half-comatose, has sunk down in her seat; ... The stinking, dusty plush seat gives no comfort, her summer dress is crumpled and she sits with sweating thighs wide apart....
>
> In the other corner sits Ester. Apparently unaffected by the heat, she holds herself upright (p. 107)

Suddenly, however, Ester vomits blood. After getting off the train she is put to bed in an hotel. She drinks a large glass of cognac after which she feels quite drunk:

> Ester thrusts her hand inside her jacket and passes it over her breasts, cups one breast in the hollow of her hand, lies down cautiously, raises her knees and thrusts her other hand under the fabric of her pyjama trousers.
>
> A drowsy feeling of security comes over her, she wets her lips, presses her head back in the soft pillow. A few moments she lies still, panting, coughs slightly, stretches herself out and closes her eyes.
>
> She rests, as if in tepid water. In soft, short spasms sleep approaches. (p. 113)

Ester's reactions are the first indication of the reduction of the emotions to something else in this film. Bergman makes much of the fact, as we shall see, that the sisters are traveling in a strange country where they do not know the language. It is not that the language is one they have heard of, but do not understand. The problem is deeper. They can make little of it as a language. They can't make out the name of the station and although Ester speaks to the elderly hotel waiter in English, German, and French, they cannot understand each other. What we have is people surrounded by an unintelligible world where they find it hard to arrive at the intelligible or meaningful. In such a world, people increasingly draw into a private world. Shared emotions, genuine expression of feelings, become a rarity, and satisfaction is sought in private sensations.

This is what we see in Ester's masturbatory satisfaction. She reduces states and emotions to sensations. She has a feeling of security, but in fact will never leave the hotel alive. Security cannot be reduced to a sensation. Whether we are secure depends on what happens to us and our strength of character. She has only the illusion of security in drawing the bedclothes about her.

Similarly, love cannot be reduced to a sensation. Sensations begin and end in the one organism. So it is with Ester's sexual sensations. No doubt they are aided by the use of imagination; a person may imagine entering into all sorts of relationships and activities. The point is that Ester does not have to actually do any of this with the commitments and risks this would involve. She can cut the story short in imagination. No risks are involved, people can be summoned and dismissed at will. Yet, the reduction of emotions to sensations in this way may take charge of a person, cutting him off from all genuine contact with those around him. Such is the case with Ester.

The hotel in which the characters find themselves seems to represent in its seediness, a growing decadence and the crumbling of an old order. There is a vulgar painting on the wall which Johan is drawn to. He discovers a room full of dwarfs who have with them trunks full of strange masks and stage clothes. They put a dress on him as they jabber incomprehensibly. Johan can't refind his room and has to relieve himself in the corridor, causing little streams to run on the red carpet. The young lad is bewildered by his surroundings. Despite the old waiter's attempt to tell him not to be afraid, he can't make much sense of what's happening.

The reduction of emotions to sensations is found not only in Ester, but in Anna too. As Anna prepares to go out, it is clear that Ester resents the fact and that despite her surface primness and denials, her attitude to her sister is sexually ambivalent. Once Anna has gone, she whimpers and moans, expressing the very humiliation which she says she will not tolerate. But Anna too has gone in search of sensation, instant gratification. She allows herself to be picked up by a waiter.

During her absence, Ester tries to console Johan, but there

is no closeness between them. Promising to draw a lovely picture for her in his room, what he in fact draws is *"a forehead, a cruel twisted mouth"* (p. 120). One of the few expressions of the genuine in the film is when the old waiter, seeing Johan watching him, beckons him and shows him a photograph of an old woman in an open coffin surrounded by friends and relations and photographs of children of varying ages. A tear runs down the old man's nose. He makes *"an expressive gesture which can mean: all dead and gone, finished. . . . Suddenly, he lays his arm around Johan's shoulders and draws him to him. The boy isn't frightened, doesn't resist; just sits there quietly, letting the old man pat him on the shoulder. For quite a long while they sit together like this"* (p. 123). Genuineness is offered by a member of an old generation, a generation of the extended family where bonds were close. But this seems to be part of what is dead, finished, gone. Where are the possibilities of genuineness to be found now?

Ester, on Anna's return, asks whether she has any conscience about her behavior. Anna will not be imposed on.

ANNA: D'you think you matter in the least? I mean, what you do or say? . . . Whoever put that notion into your head? That it's up to you to decide?

ESTER (*coldly*): You can't manage on your own.

ANNA: You think you can make my decisions for me, just like Father did. But you can't. (p. 128)

The authority of the Father's conscience has gone. Not only that, Ester's conscience, like her primness, is only a surface phenomenon. We see that what seems to be her moral indignation at her sister's behavior is a far more ambivalent interest:

ESTER: Where did you find that man?

ANNA: In the bar, just across the street.

Anna looks at her sister with a smile.

ANNA: Want to know the details?

ESTER: Answer my questions.

ANNA: D'you remember the winter ten years ago, when we were staying with Father at Lyon? And I'd been with Claude? Remember cross-examining me just the same way?

How you scratched my arm and swore you'd tell Father
if I didn't tell you all the details? (p. 129)

Ester is distressed. Anna teases her with different accounts of
her love-making with the waiter. Which one is true? It doesn't
matter any more.

ANNA: Why should I tell lies?
ESTER (*dully*): Yes, why should you tell lies?
ANNA: Though as it happens, I am.
ESTER: It doesn't matter.
Ester has crumpled into grey exhaustion, a tormented grimace.
(p. 129)

It no longer matters if the story is true as long as it excites.
Truth gives way to efficacy; an extension of Ester's solitary
pleasures. She pleads with Anna not to go to her lover, but she
cannot admit the sexual interest she has in her sister.

ESTER: It torments me.
ANNA: Does it? Why?
ESTER: Because ... Because I feel so humiliated. Don't think
     I'm jealous.
*The last in a whisper, with wide-staring eyes, her hand fum-
bling for Anna's.* (p. 130)

Anna goes to a room with her lover. We have seen already
that what she wants is instant gratification. She is well aware
that no love is involved. What we have are not emotions, but
sensations. She says to him, "How nice you are. How nice it is
we don't understand each other" (p. 133). But even here all is
not what it seems. Even the sexual adventures are ambivalent.
Are they enjoyed for themselves or are they also ways of hurt-
ing her sister? Even as she caresses her lover Anna says, "I
wish Ester were dead" (p. 133). In the end, the lover reacts to
being used. One night in bed with her lover, Anna sees the
handle of the door turn. Going up to it, she can hear Ester
weeping. She turns the key to open the door and gets back
into bed. Ester feels her way in the darkness towards the bed.
Suddenly the red bedside light is turned on. "*Anna lays her
arm round the man's neck and pretends to make herself com-*

fortable, but he moves away from her, up against the wall (p. 135). Her lover will not be used. The sisters begin to row yet again. Ester appeals to the authority of their father, but Anna will have none of it. She only obeyed him because she had to, but she is not giving that allegiance to Ester. Ester asks, "How do you want us to live, then?" (p. 136).

This is not simply Ester's question. It's Bergman's question too. Authoritarian systems are dead, but what is to be the alternative? Ester's problems are more complex. Her father was not a mere external authority. She respected him. But what earned that respect has not survived in her. There is no road back to it. Anna tells her, "In some way I can't understand, you're scared of me" (p. 130). In this respect, she is perfectly right. Ester *is* scared of what they have become, but she is also attracted by it. Ironically, her emotional ambivalence creates a parallel ambivalence even in Anna's sensuousness. Having told Ester to get out, "*Anna wildly laughing, throws herself against the wall. When the man touches her shoulder she hits him across the mouth. Her laughter turns into heavy weeping*" (p. 137).

In the corridor Ester leans against the wall, exhausted. The dwarfs come by in a procession, dressed in their grotesque masks and costumes. They seem to mock everything she is. "*Ester makes a few movements with her arms, presses her shoulders together, opens her mouth. A thin stream of blood runs quietly down over her chin, flecks her skirt and drips onto the carpet*" (p. 138). Next morning, Anna finds her lying in the corridor.

Ester has been put to bed, and Anna and Johan are getting ready to leave. Anna says she will take the boy for a quick meal before they depart, but Ester knows she is going to her lover. Ester has promised to give Johan a few words of the strange language she has managed to gather. With the aid of the old waiter she writes, "*To JOHAN, a few words of the foreign language*" (p. 139). The effort exhausts her. She tells the old man how lost she is: "We try them out, one attitude after another, and find them all meaningless. The powers are too strong for us, I mean the *monstrous* powers. You have to take care, moving among ghosts and memories" (p. 140). She says she is not afraid to die, but when convulsions almost choke her she is terrified. She covers her face with the sheet. Johan enters and lifts the sheet from her face. Ester is calmer and gives him the letter: "Johan! It's *important*, d'you understand! You must read it carefully. (*Pause*) It's all . . . It's all I . . . You'll understand" (p. 142). Anna enters businesslike. Johan does not want to go, but is dragged from under the bed. When Ester says she thinks it good that they are going, Anna replies, "No one's asked for your advice," and goes. The old waiter is left alone with Ester: "*Her face is grey, sunken. Her breath comes in short gasps. Soundlessly, on tiptoe, he leaves her*" (p. 142).

The final scene is of Anna and Johan alone in the train compartment. Johan is studying Ester's letter. Anna asks to see it, but can make nothing of the incomprehensible signs on the crinkled paper. She shrugs and gives it back to him.

> It gets darker and darker, the rain squirts down over the windowpanes. Anna opens the window and lets the water splash over her hands and face. Johan's face is pale with the effort of trying to understand the strange language. This secret message. (p. 143)

Looking back over Bergman's trilogy we might well repeat Ester's words: "We try them out, one attitude after another, and find them all meaningless" (p. 140). The god of compensations, who becomes an ugly spider god when confronted with the realities of human suffering; the attempt to find substitutes for divine authority; the reduction of truth to strategy; the reduction of emotions to sensations; the final reduction of sexual sensations to their perverted forms — Bergman presents us with all these in the context of mixed and broken memories of an order no longer with us, and of inarticulate longings for things to be different. Together they make up a "modern cosmology of the spirit." True, Johan is left with his secret message, but what is it? It is secret, not in the sense of being available but hidden, but in the sense of something which is yet to be worked out. All the characters are discontented with what they have got, but they cannot formulate what they want. That is their predicament. The trilogy begins with inscrutable grace and ends with the secret message. As I said, what we have in Bergman is a celebration of the inarticulate.

It may seem extravagent to compare Beckett's austere and economical use of language with Bergman's film trilogy which threatens, at times, to be romantically indulgent. Nevertheless, the worlds they present are not dissimilar. Sometimes Beckett's characters are more sinister; they are often happy in their mediocrity and triviality. Such a person is Winnie in *Happy Days*. Buried up to her waist in a mound of earth, she talks incessantly to her husband who is almost hidden on the other side of the mound. From time to time she rummages in a large bag, producing various objects from it which she examines carefully. One of these is a toothbrush. She tries to read the writing on the handle: "guaranteed ... genuine pure ... what? (*looks closer*) — genuine pure ... (*takes handkerchief from bodice*) — ah yes (*shakes out handkerchief*) — occasional mild migraine — (*starts wiping handle of brush*) — it comes — (*wipes*) — then goes — (*wipes mechanically*) — ah yes — (*wiping*) — many mercies — (*wiping*) — great mercies — (*stops wiping, fixed lost gaze, brokenly*) — prayers perhaps not for nought — (*pause*) first thing — (*pause*) — last thing — (*head down, resumes wiping, head up, calmed, wipes eyes, folds handkerchief, puts it back in bodice, examines handle of brush, reads*) — fully guaranteed ... genuine pure ... — (*looks closer*) ... genuine pure ... (*Takes off spectacles, lays them and brush down, gazes before her*). Old things. (*Pause*) Old eyes. (*Long Pause*)."[2]

In his first film, Bergman's title echoes the verse from Paul's epistle to the Corinthians which usually begins "For now we see through a glass darkly." An alternative translation reads: "For we look in a mirror which has puzzling reflections. But some things are certain: faith, hope, love." From film to film in Bergman's trilogy we have an increasingly darkening mirror. He leaves us with his secret message. But what things are certain? Guaranteed ... genuine pure ... *what?* Trivial though her answer is, Winnie makes an attempt to answer the question. In this trilogy of films, Bergman never does.

---

2. Samuel Beckett, *Happy Days*, p. 12.

10/SEEKING THE POEM
IN THE PAIN
– Order and Contingency
in the Poetry of R. S. Thomas

IF WE HAD ENTERED A TAVERN in the eighteenth century and listened to popular argument about what all things come to, whether there's a sense to things, whether there is Someone behind it all, we would have heard an argument which can still be heard, although on rarer occasions, today: "Someone must have started it all. It couldn't have come from nothing, could it? It can't all be chance." But the most popular religious apologetic argument of the eighteenth century would, I suspect, be seldom heard now, if at all. It went like this: "Look around you, see the order and design in nature. Note the splendor of the work. Design entails a designer." This argument, which flourished at popular and intellectual levels, is known as the Argument From Design. But even while it flourished a philosopher was bringing objections to it from which it has never recovered. I refer to David Hume's momentous work, *Dialogues Concerning Natural Religion*.

Why do we need an argument from design in the first place? Well, we have no direct proof of God's existence. We do not see God, we only see his works. How then do we get from the works to God? The answer is, by *inference*. But it was against this answer that Hume brought insuperable objections. I shall only mention two of them.

First, if in fact we only have as evidence what we see about us and have no knowledge whatever of the author of nature, we can only infer as much about the author's character as the evidence allows. If we see malice about us, then we must conclude that the author is malicious. If we see benevolence about us, we must conclude that the author is benevolent. If the character of what we see about us is mixed, as it seems to be, the creator's character must be mixed as well.

But this first point may itself concede too much, since Hume asks us to consider, in the second place, why nature should be regarded as evidence at all. Why should it be thought of as someone's work? To think in this way begs the question by anthropomorphizing nature. We look at nature, but we see gardens. We do not have to go outside nature to obtain explanations of the natural.

Nineteenth century writers built on these conclusions. Taking for granted that Hume had demonstrated the logical impossibility of inferring God's existence from the world, they turned to the question of why men had persisted for so long in believing the absurd. In their different ways Tylor, Frazer, Feuerbach, Freud, Durkheim, and Marx all attempted to account for religion as a projection of the human mind.

No attempt to understand or give expression to a religious syntax can ignore this background. For better or for worse it is our immediate intellectual inheritance, an inheritance for philosophy and poetry alike. I know of no adequate answers to Hume's objections. But what follows if we grant them? Some have thought that it follows that we must remain with the changing scenes of life, that it makes no sense any longer to seek answers to large questions, questions about the sense of all things. There is no such sense to be found. There is simply the sense of this, that, and the other thing. Sometimes, this turning from large questions may lead to preoccupation with the personal and the private. This has happened in art, and R. S. Thomas regrets it.

> But what to do? Doctors in verse
> Being scarce now, most poets
> Are their own patients, compelled to treat
> Themselves first, their complaint being
> Peculiar always.

He asks that the matter be reconsidered:

> Consider, you,
> Whose rough hands manipulate

The fine bones of a sick culture,
What areas of that infirm body
Depend solely on a poet's cure.

[*The Cure*]¹

But what is the cure and what are the conditions for receiving it? If you look for one comprehensive answer to this question in the poetry of R. S. Thomas, you will be disappointed. He does not offer one. He does present us with pictures of various conditions of men. Some of these conditions are limited and harmless, others limited and harmful. Neither category would be open to receive a poet's cure. In the first category we have those, like Thomas's Fisherman, who content themselves with specific pleasures, valuable enough in themselves, and never address themselves to larger questions:

A simple man,
He liked the crease on the water
His cast made, but had no pity
For the broken backbone
Of water or fish.

One of his pleasures, thirsty,
Was to ask a drink
At the hot farms;
Leaving with a casual thank you,
As though they owed it him.

I could have told of the living water
That springs pure.
He would have smiled then,
Dancing his speckled fly in the shallows,
Not understanding.

[*The Fisherman*]

R. S. Thomas seems to assume sometimes that if a man has not consciously posed large questions to himself then he cannot have answered them. A little later we shall hear him saying of the Peasant whom he nevertheless wants to celebrate, "There

---

1. All poems are from R. S. Thomas, *Selected Poems*, unless otherwise indicated.

is something frightening in the vacancy of his mind." But whether the mind is vacant is not determined always by whether conscious thoughts are occurring. It is determined just as often by the character of a man's activity, what shows itself in his work. The reason why some men are limited but harmless can be determined by what their lives show; in this case, by what is shown in the fisherman's attitude.

Others are limited in a way which is harmful, which eats into the souls of men. These are men who seek in things, not their sense, but their consequences. The opportunists of this world, they are at their worst, perhaps, when the old religious language is still on their lips. They have perverted that language to their own purposes. We see these portrayed in R. S. Thomas's deacons in *The Minister:*

> They chose their pastors as they chose their horses
> For hard work. But the last one died
> Sooner than they expected; nothing sinister,
> You understand, but just the natural
> Breaking of the heart beneath a load
> Unfit for horses. 'Ay, he's a good 'un,'
> Job Davies had said; and Job was a master
> Hand at choosing a nag or a pastor. . . .
>
> O, but God is in the throat of a bird;
> Ann heard Him speak, and Pantycelyn.
> God is in the sound of the white water
> Falling at Cynfal. God is in the flowers
> Spring at the foot of Olwen, and Melangell
> Felt His heart beating in the wild hare.
> Wales in fact is His peculiar home,
> Our fathers knew Him. But where is that voice now?
> Is it in the chapel vestry, where Davies is using
> The logic of the Smithfield?
>
> DAVIES
> A young 'un we want, someone young
> Without a wife. Let him learn
> His calling first, and choose after
> Among our girls, if he must marry.
> There's your girl, Pugh; or yours, Parry;

Ministers' wives they ought to be
With those white hands that are too soft
For lugging muck or pulling a cow's
Tits. But ay, he must be young.
Remember that mare of yours, John?

Too old when you bought her; the old sinner
Had had a taste of the valleys first
And never took to the rough grass
In the top fields. You could do nothing
With her, but let her go her way.
Lucky you sold her. But you can't sell
Ministers, so we must have a care
In choosing. Take my advice,
Pick someone young, and I'll soon show him
How things is managed in the hills here.

But things were not always like this, moving to an order born of a marriage between religion and prosperity, providence and prudence:

There were people here before these,
Measuring truth according to the moor's
Pitiless commentary and the wind's veto.
Out in the moor there is a bone whitening,
Worn smooth by the long dialectic
Of rain and sunlight. What has that to do
With choosing a minister? Nothing, nothing.

But if the deacons fall prey to a certain kind of opportunism, the young minister R. S. Thomas portrays falls prey to opportunism of another kind, the kind Kierkegaard calls a foreshortening of eternity. Kierkegaard speaks of such a foreshortening in his book, *Purity of Heart*. It consists essentially in the illusion of thinking that eternity can be grasped in a moment, that understanding could be compressed into a moment. A romantic example of such foreshortening would be the assumption that love could be made secure in the exchange of a glance or in a single touch. An artistic example of such foreshortening would be the assumption that significance can be possessed in a happening. Kierkegaard gives another example. He tells of a man who admired the beauty and proportions of a map. There was only one thing wrong; he did not realize that the map was to be used. So when he was put down in the heart of the country with its many miles of winding, unkept roads, dismay overtook him. He wanted to foreshorten eternity, to possess it once and for all in a gaze at the map. He was not prepared to travel.[2] R. S. Thomas finds such a foreshortening of eternity in certain aspects of Nonconformity. He quite rightly combines the foreshortening of spirituality in ecstatic moments with the romantic foreshortening of love I have already mentioned:

> I was good that night, I had the *hwyl*.
> We sang the verses of the last hymn
> Twice. We might have had a revival
> If only the organ had kept in time.
> But that was the organist's fault.
> I went to my house with the light heart
> Of one who had made a neat job
> Of pruning the branches on the tree
> Of good and evil. Llywarch came with me
> As far as the gate. Who was the girl
> Who smiled at me as she slipped by?

There is marvelous humor in the suggestion that men's coming to God depended on the organ keeping in tune. It is the Nonconformist parallel to the foreshortening of eternity Miguel de Unamuno found in the aestheticism of the Catholic religious processions he witnessed as a child, an aestheticism which led him to say, "My soul was nourished on perfume."

Yet, like Kierkegaard's map-reader, R. S. Thomas's minister is set down in the heart of the country and he finds that his *hwyl* does not travel well. It does not speak to what he sees around him. It does not speak because he does not see how the changing relentless seasons tell of God. Instead he tries to apply his university degree to these people. He holds a *seiat* and a Bible class, but no one comes. At last Morgan, the minister, becomes part of the place and keeps his silence. But the price is high, for his words cannot speak, his language is impotent:

---

2. See "Knowledge, Patience, and Faust," p. 105.

I knew it all,
Although I never pried, I knew it all.
I knew why Buddug was away from chapel.
I knew that Pritchard, the *Fron*, watered his milk.
I knew who put the ferret with the fowls
In Pugh's hen-house. I knew and pretended I didn't.
And they knew that I knew and pretended I didn't.
They listened to me preaching the unique gospel
Of love, but our eyes never met. And outside
The blood of God darkened the evening sky.

R. S. Thomas is in no doubt that Protestantism in Wales has much to answer for, that indeed it became in itself a vehicle for a foreshortening of eternity:

Is there no passion in Wales? There is none
Except in the racked hearts of men like Morgan,
Condemned to wither and starve in the cramped cell
Of thought their fathers made them.
Protestantism — the adroit castrator
Of art; the bitter negation
Of song and dance and the heart's innocent joy —
You have botched our flesh and left us only the soul's
Terrible impotence in a warm world.

Need we go on? In spite of all
His courage Morgan could not avert
His failure, for he chose to fight
With that which yields to nothing human.
He never listened to the hills'
Music calling to the hushed
Music within; but let his mind
Fester with brooding on the sly
Infirmities of the hill people.
The pus conspired with the old
Infection lurking in his breast.

In the chapel acre there is a grave,
And grass contending with the stone
For mastery of the near horizon,
And on the stone words; but never mind them:
Their formal praise is a vain gesture

Against the moor's encroaching tide.
We will listen instead to the wind's text
Blown through the roof, or the thrush's song
In the thick bush that proved him wrong,
Wrong from the start, for nature's truth
Is primary and her changing seasons
Correct out of a vaster reason
The vague errors of the flesh.

Yet, when all is said and done, this poem simply brings us back to where we began, to the question of what kind of order can be found in contingency. The answer we are offered here is the wind's text, the primary truth of nature. But this is precisely the truth to which the inheritors of Hume's legacy said we should turn. If there is no rational inference from the world to God, if the world about us is the only one available to us, that in which we live and move and have our being, then if any sense is to be found it is to be found within these boundaries. Writers like Tylor, Frazer, Feuerbach, Freud, all of whom accepted Hume's conclusions, certainly wanted to provide a substitute for religion in the lives of men. Here are Freud's words:

> And, as for the great necessities of Fate, against which there is no help, they will learn to endure with resignation. Of what use to them is the mirage of wide acres in the moon, whose harvest no one has ever yet seen? As honest smallholders on this earth they will know how to cultivate their plot in such a way that it supports them.[3]

There are plenty of instances in R. S. Thomas's poetry of salutations to those who endure with resignation. If worldly prosperity is the norm, they do not always cultivate their plot in such a way that it supports them. The support given is a kind of sense which comes from working the soil. But the movement is a downward one devoid of transcendental implications. This is brought out strikingly in a poem called *Soil:*

A field with tall hedges and a young
Moon in the branches and one star

---

3. Sigmund Freud, *The Future of an Illusion*, p. 46.

Declining westward set the scene
Where he works slowly astride the rows
Of red mangolds and green swedes
Plying mechanically his cold blade.

This is his world, the hedge defines
The mind's limits; only the sky
Is boundless, and he never looks up;
His gaze is deep in the dark soil,
As are his feet. The soil is all;
His hands fondle it, and his bones
Are formed out of it with the swedes.
And if sometimes the knife errs,
Burying itself in his shocked flesh,
Then out of the wound the blood seeps home
To the warm soil from which it came.

Despite the fact that the hedge defines the mind's limits, that man is hedged in by his rural setting, there is an affinity between him and the soil. The soil is all, and although the sky is boundless he never looks at it. Again, in *The Face*, we see how the sense is given in the endurance. An order is found, not in a transcendental realm, but in the relentless succession of the seasons, a succession which has its parallels in human life and the human soul.

He is never absent, but like a slave
Answers to the mind's bidding,
Endlessly ploughing, as though autumn
Were the one season he knew.
Sometimes he pauses to look down
To the grey farmhouse, but no signals
Cheer him; there is no applause
For his long wrestling with the angel
Of no name. I can see his eye
That expects nothing, that has the rain's
Colourlessness. His hands are broken
But not his spirit. He is like bark
Weathering on the tree of his kind.

He will go on; that much is certain.

Beneath him tenancies of the fields
Will change; machinery turn
All to noise. But on the walls
Of the mind's gallery that face
With the hills framing it will hang
Unglorified, but stern like the soil.

Similarly, places, like people, are saluted, for they too are vehicles of the relentless order of nature. Their importance is not to be assessed in terms of size and commercial importance:

Scarcely a street, too few houses
To merit the title; just a way between
The one tavern and the one shop
That leads nowhere and fails at the top
Of the short hill, eaten away
By long erosion of the green tide
Of grass creeping perpetually nearer
This last outpost of time past.

So little happens; the black dog
Cracking his fleas in the hot sun
Is history. Yet the girl who crosses
From door to door moves to a scale
Beyond the bland day's two dimensions.

Stay, then, village, for round you spins
On slow axis a world as vast
And meaningful as any poised
By great Plato's solitary mind.

[*The Village*]

If the story ended here there would be no difficulty. R. S. Thomas's poetry would be a reflection of the only thought available to those who inherit Hume's legacy. We no longer need to look upwards; there is a dignity and honor achieved here below even if its form is stern and austere. But that is only one aspect of the poetry. R. S. Thomas wants to explore other possibilities. In the end he is not content with a depiction of man as an integral part of the natural world. There are other possibilities of meaning which men have given themselves to which the poet wants to give expression:

The cow goes round and round the field,
Bored with its grass world, and in its eyes
The mute animal hunger, which you pity,
You the confirmed sentimentalist,
Playing the old anthropomorphic game.
But for the cow, it is the same world over the hedge.
No one ever teased her with pictures of flyless meadows.
Where the grass is eternally green
No matter how often the tongue bruises it,
Or the dung soils it.
But with man it is otherwise.

[*The Minister*, extract]

So men are not hedged in after all. There is talk of a somewhere else, another realm, a higher order. But how is it to be
expressed? Is there a language which expresses it? Are these
pictures of eternity teasings of the human mind? Are they
nothing more than Feuerbach suggested, projections born of
unfulfilled wishes, just as the cow's eternity would consist of
flyless meadows and the grass eternally green? In one poem we
have a fine expression of the ambiguity and ambivalence which
R. S. Thomas wants to be true to in dealing with these questions. In *A Peasant* we find the salutation of the enduring peasant we have come across already. But in the last line we have
a suggestion that further questions can be asked.

Iago Prytherch his name, though, be it allowed,
Just an ordinary man of the bald Welsh hills,
Who pens a few sheep in a gap of cloud.
Docking mangels, chipping the green skin
From the yellow bones with a half-witted grin
Of satisfaction, or churning the crude earth
To a stiff sea of clods that glint in the wind—
So are his days spent, his spittled mirth
Rarer than the sun that cracks the cheeks
Of the gaunt sky perhaps once in a week.
And then at night see him fixed in his chair
Motionless, except when he leans to gob in the fire.
There is something frightening in the vacancy of his mind.
His clothes, sour with years of sweat
And animal contact, shock the refined,

But affected, sense with their stark naturalness.
Yet this is your prototype, who, season by season
Against seige of rain and wind's attrition,
Preserves his stock, an impregnable fortress
Not to be stormed even in death's confusion.
Remember him, then, for he, too, is a winner of wars,
Enduring like a tree under the curious stars.

The relation between the enduring human and the celestial order is one of curiosity. There is no neat fit, no ready intelligibility. Only curiosity. But notice how we have moved somewhat from Hume's terms of reference. Hume's philosophical legacy is the problem of how to infer any intelligible divine order on the basis of the world we know. But in the poem the problem is reversed. The problem is how to make sense of the contingency of human life. The stars look down with curiosity. But how is it possible to speak of the stars in this way? It is not a question of any kind of inference from human affairs. The stars are given this role in a reaction to the contingency of human affairs. The stars are above us. Within a culture it is possible to find an expressive reaction in which the stars are seen as looking down. At certain times the stars may have the role of expressing stability, the endurance of an unchanging law. They do not speak in that way in R. S. Thomas's poem. There, the stars blink in astonished curiosity at the burdens men have to endure. In discussing whether it makes sense to ask for an explanation of everything, Hume argued that no hypothesis could get off the ground. One hypothesis seems as good as any other. If we conceive of God's creation by analogy with the workings of the human mind, then, argued Hume's Philo, the following hypotheses could be entertained:

This world, for ought he knows, is very faulty and imperfect, compared to a superior standard; and was only the first rude essay of some infant Deity, who afterwards abandoned it, ashamed of his lame performance; it is the work only of some dependent, inferior Deity; and is the object of derision to his superiors: it is the production of old age and dotage in some superannuated Deity; and ever since his death, has run on at adventures, from the first impulse and active force, which it received from him. . . . I cannot, for my part, think, that so wild and unsettled a system of theology is, in any respect, preferable to none at all.[4]

But what if we no longer see these conceptions of deities as hypotheses which are based inferentially on the facts? May not the deities be seen as expressive reactions to aspects of human life? We do not infer that we are the playthings of the gods, but this expressive language is sometimes the form our reaction to the contingencies of life takes. In R. S. Thomas we find a neat reversal of the emphasis found in the Argument from Design. In the traditional argument it is God who can be inferred from an order we see about us. Order in life and nature is the ground on which we can infer a divine order. But in R. S. Thomas's expressive reaction the events that befall men, having no sense, occasion bewilderment in God. The blows men suffer are seen as divine rage because the world will not yield sense:

> What is this? said God. The obstinacy
> Of its refusal to answer
> Enraged him. He struck it
> Those great blows it resounds
> With still. It glowered at
> Him, but remained dumb,
> Turning on its slow axis,
> Of pain, reflecting the year
> In its seasons . . . .
>
> [*Echoes*, extract][5]

Similarly, in *The Hand*[6] the poet tells of a struggle between God and a Hand which pleads with God to be given his name so that it may be proclaimed unambiguously to mankind. But God himself cannot see a clear vision in the mixed character of things and finally the Hand has to depart without God's blessing:

---

4. David Hume, *Dialogues Concerning Natural Religion*, p. 169.
5. R. S. Thomas, *H'M*.
6. R. S. Thomas, *Laboratories of the Spirit*.

It was a hand. God looked at it
and looked away. There was a coldness
about his heart, as though the hand
clasped it. As at the end
of a dark tunnel, he saw cities
the hand would build, engines
that it would raze them with. His sight
dimmed. Tempted to undo the joints
of the fingers, he picked it up.
But the hand, wrestled with him. 'Tell
me your name,' it cried, 'and I will write it
in bright gold. Are there not deeds
to be done, children to make, poems
to be written? The world
is without meaning, awaiting
my coming.' But God, feeling the nails
in his side, the unnerving warmth
of the contact, fought on in
silence. This was the long war with himself
always foreseen, the question not
to be answered. What is the hand
for? The immaculate conception
preceding the delivery
of the first tool? 'I let you go,'
he said, 'but without blessing.
Messenger to the mixed things
of your making, tell them I am.'

Reactions to human senselessness reaches its extreme point in
the depiction of creation in terms of malicious destruction and
the coming of Jesus as a malformation which provokes the uncontrollable laughter of God:

God looked at the eagle that looked at
the wolf that watched the jack-rabbit
cropping the grass, green and curling
as God's beard. He stepped back;
it was perfect, a self-regulating machine
of blood and faeces. One thing was missing:
he skimmed off a faint reflection of himself
in sea-water; breathed air into it,
and set the red corpuscles whirling. It was not long

before the creature had the eagle, the wolf and
the jack-rabbit squealing for mercy. Only the grass
resisted. It used it to warm its imagination
by. God took a handful of small germs,
sowing them in the smooth flesh. It was curious,
the harvest: the limbs modelled an obscene
question, the head swelled, out of the eyes came
tears of pus. There was the sound
of thunder, the loud, uncontrollable laughter of
God, and in his side like an incurred stitch, Jesus.

[Rough][7]

The curiosity of the stars, divine bewilderment in face of the
obstinate senselessness of a world of pain, the radical ambiguity
in any message brought to the mixed world of men, the near
demonic character of the divine laughter — all these are expressive reactions to the world of men. We may find some of
them hard to stomach, but that is what they are.

But are such reactions arbitrary? Certainly they are not in-
ferences or hypotheses which can be justified in terms of agreed
procedures for testing validity or truth. Nevertheless, the
reactions must give us a language which can speak to men.
Their strength resides in their ability to speak. True, they reflect certain aspects of human life and not others. Someone
might argue that the only rational response is one which gives
each aspect its due. This assumes, however, that there is some
method by which we can assess what is due to each aspect. I
know of no such method. There may be certain negative
limits which prevent the feasability of elevating the obviously
trivial, but having said that there is nothing in logic which
determines which aspect in human life is to be emphasized,
which is to be regarded as primary and which secondary.

Yet, there is a further issue to be raised. R. S. Thomas wants
to give expression in poetry to the love of God in Christianity.
This love is not simply a deification of one aspect of human
life. It tells a stranger tale. It speaks of a love which transcends
human misery and distress. In our own century those who
have tried to speak of this love in their writings include Simone

---

7. Ibid.

Weil and Thomas Merton. What they have to say is difficult, and in all conscience it must be said that many have found them too hard to swallow. It is not my task in this essay to try to give some account, as I have attempted elsewhere, of how the mixed character of human life, the very contingencies we witness, can themselves play a central role in forming a notion of divine grace in which the unavoidable is accepted as being from God. My remaining task is to ask whether any such account can be found in the poetry of R. S. Thomas. There is little doubt that he wants to put into poetry the possibility of divine love, but does he find a language in which to do so?

Whatever answer we give in the end to this question, there is no doubt that R. S. Thomas does not want to achieve a religious syntax in poetry at the cost of falsifying the facts. Above all, the facts he does not want to avoid are those of pain in human life. We find this particular insistence eloquently expressed in Hume. Against any attempt to find a neat optimistic order in nature, Hume's Philo protests,

> Look around this universe. What an immense profusion of beings, animated and organized, sensible and active! You admire this prodigious variety and fecundity. But inspect a little more narrowly these living existences, the only beings worth regarding. How hostile and destructive to each other! How insufficient all of them for their own happiness! How contemptible or odious to the spectator! The whole presents nothing but the idea of a blind nature, impregnated by a great vivifying principle, and pouring forth from her lap, without discernment or parental care, her maimed and abortive children.[8]

R. S. Thomas would be the last to ignore such facts. Many of his poems testify to the maimed and abortive victims of life and to his bewilderment in face of their testimony. The bewilderment is twofold: the bewilderment of a poet and the bewilderment of a priest. Here are two striking expressions of his awareness of the problem of evil. First, *The Island*:[9]

---

8. *Dialogues Concerning Natural Religion*, p. 211.
9. *H'M*.

And God said, I will build a church here
And cause this people to worship me,
And afflict them with poverty and sickness
In return for centuries of hard work
And patience. And its walls shall be as hard as
Their hearts, and its windows let in the light
Grudgingly, as their minds do, and the priest's words be drowned
By the wind's caterwauling. All this I will do,

Said God, and watch the bitterness in their eyes
Grow, and their lips suppurate with
Their prayers. And their women shall bring forth
On my altars, and I will choose the best
Of them to be thrown back into the sea.

And that was only on one island.

The second poem, *No*:

> And one said, This man can sing;
> Let's listen to him. But the other,
> Dirt on his mind, said, No, let's
> Queer him. And the first, being weak,
> Consented. So the Thing came
> Nearer him, and its breath caused
> Him to retch, and none knew why.
> But he rested for one long month,
> And after began to sing
> For gladness, and the Thing stood,
> Letting him, for a year, for two;
> Then put out its raw hand
> And touched him, and the wound took
> Over, and the nurses wiped off
> The poetry from his cracked lips.

The poet wishes it were otherwise, but his petition is not
granted. The truth will not be denied:

> And I standing in the shade
> Have seen it a thousand times
> Happen: first theft, then murder;
> Rape; the rueful acts
> Of the blind hand. I have said

New prayers, or said the old
In a new way. Seeking the poem
In the pain, I have learned
Silence is best, paying for it
With my conscience. I am eyes
Merely, witnessing virtue's
Defeat; seeing the young born
Fair, knowing the cancer
Awaits them. One thing I have asked
Of the disposer of the issues
Of life: that truth should defer
To beauty. It was not granted.

[*Petition*][10]

In the face of the large questions he has asked himself, that is R. S. Thomas's task — seeking the poem in the pain. Insofar as the poem he seeks is one which expresses the Christian God's answer of love to a world of pain, there are only a few authentic moments. In *Judgement Day*, a moving confession of wrongs committed in life leads to the petition,

Lord, breathe once more
On that sad mirror,
Let me be lost
In mist for ever
Rather than own such bleak reflections.
Let me go back on my two knees
Slowly to undo
The knot of life
That was tied there.

In *St. Julian and the Leper* there is expression of a spontaneity of love which "Our science has disinfected." But attempts to be more positive on a larger scale fail. The strained analogy between a performance by Kreisler and the crucifixion of Christ in *The Musician*[11] needs a falsification of facts in an attempt to make it work. It simply is not true that no one dared to interrupt at the Cross "Because it was himself that he played." On the contrary, he was reviled by the majority, and

---

10. Ibid.
11. R. S. Thomas, *Tares*.

the silence of the believers was one of dismay, not of awe. Again, the attempt in *Alive* to show how God is present in all things is simply pedantic, a tired language which no longer speaks.

There are four poems, however, where it seems to me that R. S. Thomas's religious reflections deepen. Perhaps in *Kneeling* we have little more than the prefatory comment that "The meaning is in the waiting." But more is attempted in *Via Negativa* and *Making*. Here the poet moves away from the idea of God's power as an extension of human power on a grand scale. Philosophers often pose evil's problem for God in the following terms: God cannot be both omnipotent and good. If he is omnipotent then he doesn't want to do anything about evil. If he wants to do something about evil, then since he doesn't it must be because he is restricted in some way. But Simone Weil offers us a different reading of God's creation. She sees it not as an act of power in the sense I have referred to but as an act of divine withdrawal. She identifies God's power with his love. Love's acts are acts of dying to the self. We have hints of this in R. S. Thomas. Thus in *Making* the creation of man is described as follows:

> I slept and dreamed
> Of a likeness, fashioning it,
> When I woke, to a slow
> Music; in love with it
> For itself, giving it freedom
> To love me; risking the disappointment.
>
> [*Making*, extract][12]

In *Via Negativa* and in *Somewhere*, the waiting on this love is conceived, not as assenting to a set of propositions, propositions for which Hume raised so many problems, but as the spirit in which we travel. Thus we are told in *Via Negativa*,

> Why no! I never thought other than
> That God is that great absence
> In our lives, the empty silence

---

12. *H'M*.

Within, the place where we go
Seeking, not in hope to
Arrive or find.

[*Via Negativa*, extract][13]

And again in *Somewhere*:[14]

Something to bring back to show
you have been there: a lock of God's
hair, stolen from him while he was
asleep; a photograph of the garden
of the spirit. As has been said,
the point of travelling is not
to arrive, but to return home
laden with pollen you shall work up
into the honey the mind feeds on.

What are our lives but harbours
we are continually setting out
from, airports at which we touch
down and remain in too briefly
to recognize what it is they remind
us of? And always in one
another we seek the proof
of experiences it would be worth dying for.

Surely there is a shirt of fire
this one wore, that is hung up now
like some rare fleece in the hall of heroes?
Surely these husbands and wives
have dipped their marriages in a fast
spring? Surely there exists somewhere,
as the justification for our looking for it,
the one light that can cast such shadows?

But these are hints, beginnings of a deeper theme, no more. I do not pretend either that they are among the most memorable of R. S. Thomas's poems. What we remember is the ambiguity, the enduring ambivalence born of the attempt to find love in pain. R. S. Thomas introduces the ambiguity and ambiva-

---

13. Ibid.
14. *Laboratories of the Spirit.*

lence even into the heart of Christianity, the elements of the
Eucharist:

> The people rise
> And walk to the churches'
> Stone lanterns, there to kneel
> And eat the new bread
> Of love, washing it down
> With the sharp taste
> Of blood they will shed.
>
> [*Christmas*, extract][15]

R. S. Thomas refuses to etherealize faith. If faith is real it must
speak to the most austere conditions of human life; to the two
cronies depicted in *Look*, for example:

> Mildew and pus and decay
> They deal in, and feed on mucous
> And wind, diet of a wet land.
>
> [*Look*, extract]

R. S. Thomas concludes with the insistence,

> We must dip belief
> Not in dew nor in the cool fountain
> Of beech buds, but in seas
> Of manure through which they squelch
> To the bleakness of their assignations.
>
> [*Look*, extract]

When we look back over the corpus of R. S. Thomas's poetry we remember more than anything the limits and limitations
within which faith struggles to find expression. The limits and
limitations come from nature and from men's dealings with
one another. In the well-known *Meet the Family* we see the
terrible order which may be imposed on a family by the dead
being present in the form of absence:

> John All and his lean wife,
> Whose forced complicity gave life
> To each loathed foetus, stare from the wall,
> Dead not absent. The night falls.

15. R. S. Thomas, *Not That He Brought Flowers*.

Yet, the explicitness of the poem detracts somewhat from the horror it depicts. Far more terrible, because not stated explicitly, is the depiction of life *On the Farm:*

> There was Dai Puw. He was no good.
> They put him in the fields to dock swedes,
> And took the knife from him, when he came home
> At late evening with a grin
> Like the slash of a knife on his face.
>
> There was Llew Puw, and he was no good.
> Every evening after the ploughing
> With the big tractor he would sit in his chair,
> And stare into the tangled fire garden,
> Opening his slow lips like a snail.
>
> There was Huw Puw, too. What shall I say?
> I have heard him whistling in the hedges
> On and on, as though winter
> Would never again leave those fields,
> And all the trees were deformed.
>
> And lastly there was the girl:
> Beauty under some spell of the beast.
> Her pale face was the lantern
> By which they read in life's dark book
> The shrill sentence: God is love.

As I said earlier, in face of a world such as this, the poem that comes out of the pain is often a poem of bewilderment, sometimes the bewilderment of a priest. But before leaving the poetry of R. S. Thomas it must be said that the bewilderment sometimes gives way to impatience and the impatience to nastiness. In the two poems we have just discussed the nastiness depicted is that of John All and the Puw brothers, but in other cases the nastiness is in the poetry itself. In *The Country Clergy*[16] R. S. Thomas says that the venerable priests who are not recognized in terms of the order of this world will be recognized in terms of eternity's order. So far, so good. But he also says of the priests:

---

16. R. S. Thomas, *Poetry for Supper.*

> And yet their skulls,
> Ripening over so many prayers,
> Toppled into the same grave
> With oafs and yokels . . .

and expresses the hope that "God in his time/Or out of time will correct this." But why does it need correcting? Is the priest to think of himself as superior to oafs and yokels? Again, in an extremely harsh poem, *The Calling*,[17] R. S. Thomas tells the priest to test his vocation in the presence of people such as these:

> Share their distraught
> joy at the dropping of their inane
> children. Test your belief
>
> in spirit on their faces staring
> at you, on beauty's surrender
> to truth, on the soul's selling
> of itself for a corner
>
> by the body's fire. Learn the thinness
> of the window that is
> between you and life, and how
> the mind cuts itself if it goes through.

Why must the birth of children be described as a dropping, and the children themselves be described as inane? Here, the poem is not found in the pain, but adds to it.

We are now in a position to answer the main question we asked about R. S. Thomas's poetry. Does he find a poem in the pain, one which expresses religion's answer to the woes of the world? Despite hints here and there, the final answer must be, No. Perhaps the answer is negative, not only because of the reasons I have given, but because, obsessed by the pain he sees around him, R. S. Thomas finds little which expresses joy. Praise seems foreign to his poetry, and on the rare occasions it appears there is a desperation about it which robs it of the purity it has sometimes had in the mouths of men. Take, for

---

17. *Laboratories of the Spirit.*

example, *The Cry*, where the poet tries to give us some measure of reassurance:

> Don't think it was all hate
> That grew there; love grew there, too,
> Climbing by small tendrils where
> The warmth fell from the eyes' blue
>
> Flame. Don't think even the dirt
> And the brute ugliness reigned
> Unchallenged. Among the fields
> Sometimes the spirit, enchained
>
> So long by the gross flesh, raised
> Suddenly there its wild note of praise.

The praise is wild, desperate. The title of the poem, after all, is not *Praise*, but *The Cry*. In his Introduction to the *Selected Poems of Edward Thomas*, R. S. Thomas says, "Edward Thomas wrote in the English language; almost all his poems were about the English country-side. Yet one Welshman, at least, toys with the idea that the melancholy and wry whimsicality, the longing to make the glimpsed good place permanent, which appear in Thomas' verse, may have had a Welsh source."[18] R. S. Thomas writes about the Welsh countryside in the English language. Here we find not melancholy, but often a hate, a hate obviously connected with his savage view of Wales, a Wales in which, nevertheless, the struggle for meaning must go on. This would be a theme for a lecture in itself, so I do no more than mention it. R. S. Thomas says of Edward Thomas: "Somewhere beyond the borders of Thomas' mind, there was a world he never could quite come at. Many of his best poems are a faithful recording of his attempts to do so."[19] It must be said that that world has receded further in the poetry of R. S. Thomas, although in his Eisteddfod lecture *Abercuawg* he does grapple further with the sense in which something may be present in the form of absence.[20] But what

---

18. *Selected Poems of Edward Thomas*, p. 11.
19. Ibid.
20. R. S. Thomas, *Abercuawg*.

implications has this answer for the poetry? Does it mean that he merits the verdict he himself depicts in *Death Of A Poet*?[21]

> Laid now on his smooth bed
> For the last time, watching dully
> Through heavy eyelids the day's colour
> Widow the sky, what can he say
> Worthy of record, the books all open,
> Pens ready, the faces, sad,
> Waiting gravely for the tired lips
> To move once — what can he say?
>
> His tongue wrestles to force one word
> Past the thick phlegm; no speech, no phrases
> For the day's news, just the one word 'sorry';
> Sorry for the lies, for the long failure
> In the poet's war; that he preferred
> The easier rhythms of the heart
> To the mind's scansion; that now he dies
> Intestate, having nothing to leave
> But a few songs, cold as stones
> In the thin hands that asked for bread.

We do not know whether R. S. Thomas would judge himself in this way. In any case there is a desirable asymmetry between first person and third person judgments in these matters. That is certainly not how we should see his poems. True, he has given us no entirely satisfactory religious syntax in verse. To what extent is such a syntax possible in the English language today? But, then, R. S. Thomas has accepted no easy substitutes, no pat replies, and the integrity of his poetic voice is in the expression of our impotence where these matters are concerned. He also shows us those for whom such questions do not arise. He shows us the opportunists and the foreshorteners of eternity. He shows us those who endure with resignation, and he salutes them. Yet he does not turn from the larger questions of order and contingency, although he may think that in the end we have no longer any satisfactory answer to

---

21. *Poetry for Supper.*

them. As in *The Combat*,[22] his struggle with language goes on:

> You have no name.
> We have wrestled with you all
> day, and now night approaches,
> the darkness from which we emerged
> seeking; and anonymous
> you withdraw, leaving us nursing
> our bruises, our dislocations.
>
> For the failure of language
> there is no redress. The physicists
> tell us your size, the chemists
> the ingredients of your
> thinking. But who you are
> does not appear, nor why
> on the innocent marches
> of vocabulary you should choose
> to engage us, belabouring us
> with your silence. We die, we die
> with the knowledge that your resistance
> is endless at the frontier of the great poem.

Poetry breaks the thin window between R. S. Thomas and life, and we see how his mind cuts itself as it goes through.

---

22. *Laboratories of the Spirit*.

PHILOSOPHICAL
BIBLIOGRAPHY

Camus, Albert. *The Myth of Sisyphus and Other Essays*. Trans. Justin O'Brien. New York: Vintage Books, 1959.

Cavell, Stanley. "Ending the Waiting Game," *Must We Mean What We Say?* New York: Scribner, 1969.

Dilman, Ilham and D. Z. Phillips. *Sense and Delusion*. London: Routledge & Kegan Paul, 1971.

Foot, Philippa. *Virtues and Vices*. Oxford: Basil Blackwell, 1978.

Freud, Sigmund. *The Origins of Psycho-Analysis: Letters to Wilhelm Fliess, Drafts and Notes, 1887-1902*. Ed. Marie Bonaparte, Anna Freud, and Ernst Krist. Trans. Eric Mosbacher and James Strachey. London: Imago, 1954.

Hare, R. M. *The Language of Morals*. London: Oxford University Press, 1961.

Freedom and Reason. London: Oxford University Press, 1963.

Holland, R. F. "The Miraculous," *Religion and Understanding*. Ed. D. Z. Phillips. Oxford: Basil Blackwell, 1967.

Hume, David. *Dialogues Concerning Natural Religion*. Indianapolis: Bobbs-Merril, n.d.

Jones, Joe R. "Some Remarks on Authority and Revelation in Kierkegaard," *The Journal of Religion* 57, no. 3 (July 1977), 232-251.

Kamenka, Eugene. *Marxism and Ethics*. London: Macmillan & Co., 1969.

Kierkegaard, Søren. *Purity of Heart*. Trans. Douglas Steere. New York: Harper Torchbooks, 1956.

Malcolm, Norman. *Ludwig Wittgenstein: A Memoir*. London: Oxford University Press, 1958.

Melden, A. I. *Rights and Right Conduct*. Oxford: Basil Blackwell, 1959.

Rights and Persons. Oxford: Basil Blackwell, 1977.

Mundle, C. W. K. *A Critique of Linguistic Philosophy*. Oxford: Clarendon Press, 1970.

Phillips, D. Z. "Does It Pay To Be Good?" *Proceedings of the Aristotelian Society*, 1964-1965, 45-60.

Phillips, D. Z. and H. O. Mounce. "On Morality's Having a Point," *Philosophy* 40 (1965), 308-319.

Phillips, D. Z. and H. S. Price. "Remorse without Repudiation," *Analysis* 28 (1967), 18-20.

Phillips, D. Z. and H. O. Mounce. *Moral Practices*. London: Routledge & Kegan Paul, 1970.

Sartre, Jean-Paul. *Literary and Philosophical Essays*. Trans. Annette Michelson. London: Rider, 1955.

Stocks, J. L. *Morality and Purpose*. Ed. with an Introduction by D. Z. Phillips. London: Routledge & Kegan Paul, 1969.

Weil, Simone. *Gravity and Grace*. Trans. Emma Crauford. London: Routledge & Kegan Paul, 1952.

"Concerning the 'Our Father'," *Waiting On God*. Trans. Emma Crauford. London: Fontana, 1959.

Winch, Peter. *The Idea of a Social Science*. London: Routledge & Kegan Paul, 1958.

"The Universalizability of Moral Judgments," *Ethics and Action*. London: Routledge & Kegan Paul, 1972.

"Moral Integrity," *Ethics and Action*.

Wittgenstein, Ludwig. *Tractatus Logico-Philosophicus*. Trans. D.F. Pears and B.F. McGuinness. London: Routledge & Kegan Paul, 1961.

Philosophical Investigations. Trans. G.E.M. Anscombe. Oxford: Basil Blackwell, 1953.

LITERARY BIBLIOGRAPHY

Alley, Robert. *Last Tango in Paris*. London: Pan Books, n.d.

Auchincloss, Louis. "Edith Wharton and Her New Yorks," *Edith Wharton: A Collection of Critical Essays*. Ed. Irving Howe. Englewood Cliffs, N.J.: Prentice-Hall, 1962.

Bair, Deidre. *Samuel Beckett*. London: Jonathan Cape, 1978.

Beckett, Samuel. *Proust*. New York: Grove Press. 1957.

Endgame. New York: Grove Press, 1958.

Happy Days. London: Faber & Faber, 1970.

Waiting for Godot. London: Faber & Faber, 1977.

Bergman, Ingmar. *Three Films*. Trans. Paul Britten Austin. New York: Grove Press, 1970.

Coxe, Louis O. "What Edith Wharton Saw In Innocence" *Edith Wharton: A Collection of Critical Essays*.

Dostoyevsky, Fyodor. *The Gambler/Bobok/A Nasty Story*. Trans. Jessie Coulson. Harmondsworth: Penguin Books, 1976.

Esslin, Martin. *The Theatre of the Absurd*. Harmondsworth: Penguin Books, 1977.

Goethe, Johann Wolfgang. *Faust/Part One*. Trans. and ed. Philip Wayne. Harmondsworth: Penguin Books, 1976.

Hardy, Thomas. *Tess of the D'Urbervilles*. London: Macmillan & Co., 1912.

Howe, Irving (Ed.) *Edith Wharton: A Collection of Critical Essays*. Englewood Cliffs, N.J.: Prentice-Hall, 1962.

"A Reading of The House of Mirth," *Edith Wharton: A Collection of Critical Essays*.

Ionesco, Eugene. "Dans les armes de la ville," *Cahiers de la Compagnie Madeleine Renaud — Jean-Louis Barrault*, Paris, No. 20, Oct. 1957.

Jong, Erica. *Fear of Flying*. New York: New American Library, 1975.

Lawrence, D. H. "Morality and the Novel," *Selected Literary Criticism*. Ed. Anthony Beal. London: Heinemann, 1955.

Marlowe, Christopher. *The Complete Poems and Plays*. Ed. E. D. Pendry. London: Dent, 1976.

Nevius, Blake. "On the Age of Innocence," *Edith Wharton: A Collection of Critical Essays*.

Sophocles. *Oedipus the King*. Trans. Bernard M. W. Knox. New York: Pocket Books, 1972.

Spiers, Logan. "Tolstoy and Chekhov: The Death of Ivan Ilych and A Dreary Story," *The Oxford Review*, No. 8, 1968, pp. 81-93.

Thomas, Edward. *Selected Poems*. Selected with an Introduction by R. S. Thomas. London: Faber & Faber, 1964.

Thomas, R. S. *Selected Poems 1946-68*, London: Hart-Davis, 1973.
Poetry For Supper. London: Hart-Davis, 1964.
Tares. London: Hart-Davis, 1964.
Not That He Brought Flowers. London: Hart-Davis, 1968.
H'm. London: Macmillan & Co., 1972.
Laboratories of the Spirit. London: Macmillan & Co., 1975.
Abercuawg. Llandysul, Dyfed: Gomer Press, 1976.

Tolstoy, Leo. *The Death of Ivan Ilych and Other Stories*. Trans. Alymer Maude. New York: Signet Classic, New American Library, 1960.
Anna Karenina. Trans. with an Introduction by Rosemary Edmonds. Harmondsworth: Penguin Books, 1956.

Trilling, Lionel. "The Morality of Inertia," *Edith Wharton: A Collection of Critical Essays*.

Wharton, Edith. *The Age of Innocence*. London: Lehmann, 1953.
The House of Mirth. London: Lehmann, 1953.
The Custom of the Country. London: Lehmann, 1954.
Ethan Frome. London: Macmillan & Co., 1911.
A Backward Glance. London: Constable, 1972.

Wilson, Edmund. "Justice to Edith Wharton," *Edith Wharton: A Collection of Critical Essays*.

INDEX

Argument from Design, 165–166, 177.

Auchincloss, Louis, 19, 20.

Bair, Deirdre, 127.

Beckett, Samuel, 5, 8, 115, 119–132, 164; *Waiting for Godot*, 119–127; *Happy Days*, 164.

Bergman, Ingmar, 7, 133–164; *Through A Glass Darkly*, 134–150; *Winter Light*, 150–157; *The Silence*, 157–163.

Camus, Albert, 115–117.

Carlyle, Thomas, 98.

Cavell, Stanley, 129.

Celestial Order, 176.

Chekhov, Anton, 53, 54, 57, 61, 120; *A Dreary Story*, 51.

Coxe, Louis, 21, 24, 27.

Demonic, the, 104.

Descartes, René, 121.

Dilman, Ilham, 66–81; account of *The Death of Ivan Ilych*, 67–69; criticism of the account, 70–71.

Dostoyevsky, Fyodor, 43, 44.

Duff, Anthony, 117.

Emotions (and Sensations), 158f.

Esslin, Martin, 113–132.

Faulkner, William, 39.

Faust (and Faustus), 4, 89–112.

Feuerbach, Ludwig, 172, 175.

Foot, Philippa, 34.

Freud, Sigmund, 4, 82–88, 172.

Frazer, James, 172.

Genet, Jean, 128.

Gessner, Niklaus, 128.

God, 6–7, 134, 135, 168–189; and compensation, 149, 155; and creation, 183; existence of, 153; and the future, 4–5, 91–97; and grace, 148–149; and love, 140–142, 179; and madness, 144–147; God's silence, 151f.

Goethe, Johann Wolfgang von, 4, 89–112.

Hardy, Thomas, 45, 46, 49, 50.

Hare, R. M., 33.

Holland, R. F., 95–98.

Howe, Irving, 26.

Hume, David, 165, 166, 176, 180.

Huxley, Aldous, 63.

Hwyl, 170.

Identity, 122–127.

Inarticulateness, 137–138, 144.

Ionesco, Eugène, 115.

Jones, Joe R., 124.

Kamenka, Eugene, 29.

Kierkegaard, Søren, 99, 105, 123, 124, 169.

Language, and logic, 130; as inherently inadequate, 113, 127–129; struggle with, 190.

Lawrence, D. H., 59, 60, 91.

Limits, means-ends distinction, 30–31; of moral endeavor, 37f.; on human action, 30f. See also Morality.

Literature, (reminders from), 1, 9, 19f., 37f., 70f., 85f., 101f., 119f.

Magic, 102f.

Malcolm, Norman, 58.

Marlowe, Christopher, 4, 89–112.

Marshall, Sandra, 117.

Mauriac, Francois, 59.

Meaning, in face of death, 51–63, 76–79; of life, 5, 65–67, 79–81; loss of, 1, 6, 118, 152.

Melden, A. I., 35.

Moral Dilemmas, 38–39.

Moral Endeavor, (limits of), 37f.

Moral Philosophy, (and the novel), 9–29.

Morality, as additional principle of discrimination, 31f.; as guide to human conduct, 31–32; and limiting situations, 2, 39–42; limitations of character, 42–45; limitations of life's contingencies, 45–46; consequences of ignoring these limitations, 47–49; and prescriptivism, 33–34; and human good and harm, 34–35; as moral deliberation within a moral community, 35–36.

Mounce, H. O., 28, 38, 93.

Mundle, C. W. K., 29.

Mystical Experience, 132.

Nevius, Blake, 14, 15.

Occult, the, 136, 149.

Oedipus Complex, 4, 82–88.

Opportunism, 169.

Optimism, 2, 36–37, 41.

Passion, the, 156–157.

Patience, 99–112; and intellectual inquiry, 101–104; and love, 104–107; and morality, 107–111.

Perspectives, (on life), 3; erosion of, 1, 6, 8, 24f., 113–119.

Philosophy, as obscuring mirror, 1–3; presuppositions of, 1–3, 49, 65f., 89–97; and literature, 4, 9, 10.

Price, H. S., 38.

Problem of Evil, 180–182.

Promising, 123, 124.

Protestantism (in Wales), 171.

Providence (and prosperity), 169.

Rationality, abstracted concept of, 10f.; artificiality of, 22f; and assumptions of literary critics, 14f., 51f; characterization of,

12f; generalization of, 4, 5; and means-end distinction, 30–31; single system of, 2, 5, 130–132; and values, 2, 3.

Reasonable Man, 12f.

Reductionism, 6, 7, 132–163.

Religion, and compensation, 7; and the novel, 58–59.

Resignation, 172, 173.

Romanticism, 169f.

Sartre, Jean Paul, 59, 60, 116, 117.

Sims, D. L., 10, 85, 111.

Sophocles, 82–88; and *Oedipus Rex*, 4, 82–88; and identity, 85–86; and fate, 86–88.

Speirs, Logan, 51–63; his criticism of *The Death of Ivan Ilych*, 51–56.

Stocks, J. L., 31, 80.

Theatre of the Absurd, 5, 113–131.

Thomas, Edward, 188.

Thomas, R. S., 165–190.

Tolstoy, Leo, 3, 51–63, 67–81; *The Death of Ivan Ilych*, 51–63.

Trilling, Lionel, 17.

Tylor, E. B., 172.

Unattainable Good, relevance of, 45.

Values, 2; and the critics, 62, 63; heterogeneity of, 3, 5, 6, 49, 50.

Waiting, 119–122.

Weil, Simone, 72, 75, 77, 183.

Wharton, Edith, 2, 10–29; *The Age of Innocence*, 14f.; *The Custom of the Country*, 23; *The House of Mirth*, 26; discussion of critics of, 14f.

Wilson Edmund, 16, 17.

Winch, Peter, 9, 13, 32, 48, 86.

Wittgenstein, Ludwig, 58, 74, 90, 129–131.